Haunted Ships & Boats

Nautical Nightmares and Paranormal Encounters at Sea

By Lee Brickley

Copyright @ Lee Brickley 2023

Contents:

Introduction..5

The Flying Dutchman: The Legendary Phantom Ship.......................7

The Queen Mary: Luxury Liner Turned Haunted Attraction........13

The USS Hornet: The Haunted Aircraft Carrier.....................21

The Mary Celeste: The Ultimate Maritime Mystery................27

The Star of India: A Haunting Voyage................................33

The HMS Victory: Naval Battles and Restless Spirits.............39

The Octavius: Frozen Ghost Ship of the Arctic.....................45

The Lady Lovibond: The Ghost Ship of Goodwin Sands..............51

The SS Valencia: Graveyard of the Pacific's Haunted Wreck........57

 The Princess Augusta: The Palatine Light's Fiery Origins............65

The Ourang Medan: A Cryptic SOS and Ghostly Crew...................71

The HMS Eurydice: The Haunted Warship of the Solent................77

The Carroll A. Deering: The Bermuda Triangle's Ghost Ship........83

The SS Watertown: Faces in the Waves..89

The Admiral Nelson: The Haunted Tall Ship.....................................95

The SS Great Eastern: Iron Leviathan's Phantom Passengers...103

The MV Joyita: The Pacific's Vanishing Ghost Ship...................109

The Young Teazer: The Fiery Spectre of Mahone Bay..................115

The Eliza Battle: The Burning Ghost of the Tombigbee River...121

The Zebu: The Cursed Brigantine of the Mersey............................127

The USS Constellation: Haunted Baltimore Harbor......................133

Afterword...139

Introduction

Welcome aboard "Haunted Ships & Boats: Nautical Nightmares and Paranormal Encounters at Sea," a thrilling journey into the mysterious world of ghostly vessels and eerie phenomena that have haunted seafarers for centuries. From the legendary Flying Dutchman to the tragic tale of the Mary Celeste, this book invites you to delve into the fascinating histories and chilling stories of 21 of the world's most haunted ships and boats.

Throughout these pages, you'll encounter the restless spirits that linger on decommissioned warships, the ghostly apparitions that haunt historic sailing vessels, and the chilling mysteries that surround abandoned schooners. Each chapter offers a captivating exploration of a unique maritime haunting, complete with historical context, spine-tingling eyewitness accounts, and the eerie legends that persist to this day.

Discover the haunted past of the majestic Queen Mary, a retired ocean liner turned paranormal hotspot, and delve into the chilling history of the USS Hornet, a warship with a dark legacy. Uncover the tragic story of the SS Valencia and the ghostly sightings of lifeboats that continue to haunt the waters of the Pacific Northwest.

As you embark on this voyage into the unknown, you'll not only uncover the supernatural secrets hidden within the hulls of these vessels but also explore the depths of human fascination with the paranormal. From the mysterious disappearances in the Bermuda Triangle to the fiery apparitions of doomed steamboats, "Haunted Ships & Boats" will leave you enthralled and perhaps even a little unnerved.

Whether you're an avid paranormal enthusiast or a curious reader seeking a thrilling adventure, this book promises to captivate, entertain, and inspire your imagination. So, batten down the hatches and prepare to set sail on a nautical journey like no other, as we navigate the haunted waters of history's most enigmatic vessels. Will you brave the storm and uncover the chilling secrets that lie beneath the surface?

The Flying Dutchman: The Legendary Phantom Ship

A stormy night on the high seas, the wind howling and waves crashing against the hull of a ship sailing through the darkness. Suddenly, out of the mist, a ghostly vessel appears, its tattered sails illuminated by an eerie glow. The terrified crew gazes upon the phantom ship, knowing that their encounter with the legendary Flying Dutchman is a harbinger of doom. This haunting image has captivated the imaginations of seafarers and landlubbers alike for centuries, as the tale of the cursed ship and its tormented captain weaves its way through maritime folklore and into the annals of popular culture.

To understand the allure of the Flying Dutchman, we must first delve into its origins, tracing its journey from nautical myth to enduring symbol of the supernatural. The legend of the cursed ship is believed to have its roots in the 17th-century Dutch Golden Age, a period of unprecedented maritime prosperity, during which the Dutch East India Company established a vast trading empire that spanned the globe. The Dutch were renowned for their exceptional seamanship and navigation skills, with their ships venturing into uncharted waters in search of new trade routes and exotic goods.

It was during this era of exploration and adventure that the story of the Flying Dutchman was born, inspired by the exploits of a real-life Dutch captain named Hendrick van der Decken. Van der Decken was a skilled and daring mariner, known for his stubborn refusal to back down in the face of adversity. According to the legend, he set sail from Amsterdam in 1641, bound for the Far East with a cargo of valuable goods. As his ship approached the treacherous waters of the Cape of Good Hope, a storm began to rage, its fierce winds and towering waves threatening to send the vessel to a watery grave.

Undeterred by the tempest, Van der Decken was determined to round the cape and continue his voyage, even as his crew pleaded with him to turn back. As the storm intensified, the desperate captain made a fateful vow, swearing that he would complete his journey, even if it took him until Judgment Day. It was this reckless oath that sealed his fate, as the heavens responded with a crack of thunder and a flash of lightning, condemning the ship and its crew to roam the seas for eternity, never to find safe harbour.

Since that ill-fated voyage, tales of the Flying Dutchman have proliferated, with countless sailors claiming to have witnessed the ghostly ship on its eternal journey. The accounts often share common elements, describing a spectral vessel with tattered sails and a ghastly glow, appearing out of the mist or darkness, and disappearing just as suddenly, leaving behind an overwhelming sense of dread. In some cases, the phantom ship is said to signal other vessels, attempting to pass on letters or messages from the long-deceased crew, only to vanish when approached.

One of the earliest recorded sightings of the Flying Dutchman dates back to 1795, when a British naval officer named Captain John MacDonald was sailing off the coast of Madagascar. He reported encountering a mysterious ship under full sail, with its sails and rigging glowing a ghostly white. As his crew watched in amazement, the apparition disappeared, leaving them convinced they had witnessed the legendary phantom ship.

In another famous encounter, the future King George V of England was serving as a midshipman aboard the HMS

Bacchante during a voyage to Australia in 1881. As the ship rounded the Cape of Good Hope, the young prince and several other crew members claimed to have seen the Flying Dutchman, its red light glowing ominously in the darkness. Tragically, the sailor who first spotted the apparition fell from the rigging and died later that day, further fueling the belief that an encounter with the phantom ship was a harbinger of doom.

The legend of the Flying Dutchman has also been immortalised in literature, art, and music, testifying to its enduring appeal as a symbol of the supernatural. The 19th-century poet Samuel Taylor Coleridge drew inspiration from the tale in his epic poem "The Rime of the Ancient Mariner," in which a cursed ship is condemned to roam the seas after killing an albatross, a symbol of good fortune. The ghostly vessel is described as a "spectre-ship," with its crew of lifeless sailors serving as a chilling reminder of the consequences of defying the natural order.

The tale of the haunted ship has also found its way onto the stage, most notably in Richard Wagner's opera "Der fliegende Holländer," which premiered in 1843. Wagner's adaptation of the legend centres on the story of a tormented captain, cursed to sail the seas for eternity after making a blasphemous vow. The opera combines elements of the supernatural with a tragic love story, as the captain's salvation ultimately hinges on the unwavering devotion of a woman named Senta.

The enduring fascination with the Flying Dutchman can be attributed in part to its symbolic resonance, as the phantom ship serves as a powerful metaphor for the human condition. The image of the cursed vessel, eternally seeking safe harbour but never able to find it, reflects the existential struggle to find meaning and purpose in a world that can often seem capricious and unforgiving. The story of the tormented captain, driven by ambition and hubris to defy the forces of nature, serves as a cautionary tale, reminding us of the dangers of pride and the limits of human endeavour.

In addition to its metaphorical significance, the legend of the Flying Dutchman also taps into a primal human fascination with the unknown and the inexplicable. The vast, unfathomable depths of the ocean have long been a source of mystery and wonder, giving rise to countless myths and legends that seek to make sense of the seemingly supernatural phenomena encountered at sea. From the eerie glow of St. Elmo's fire to the uncanny appearance of ghostly ships, these maritime mysteries capture our imagination, inviting us to ponder the limits of our understanding and confront our deepest fears.

As we explore the haunted waters of history's most enigmatic vessels, the story of the Flying Dutchman serves as a reminder of the enduring power of myth and the human desire to seek answers in the face of the unexplained. While the truth behind the legendary phantom ship may never be fully unravelled, its haunting image will continue to captivate our collective imagination, as we gaze out into the misty horizon and wonder what mysteries lie just beyond our sight.

The Queen Mary: Luxury Liner Turned Haunted Attraction

Majestic and awe-inspiring, the RMS Queen Mary was once the epitome of luxury, elegance, and sophistication, a floating palace that ferried the rich and famous across the Atlantic during the golden age of ocean travel. Today, this magnificent vessel has found a new life as a floating hotel and tourist attraction, drawing visitors from around the world with its rich history, stunning architecture, and an undeniable air of mystery. For within the opulent halls and staterooms of this retired ocean liner, a host of spectral residents are said to roam, their restless spirits bearing witness to the ship's storied past and the countless lives that intersected within its grand confines.

Launched in 1934, the Queen Mary was the largest and fastest ship of its time, a marvel of engineering and design that represented the pinnacle of British craftsmanship. With its sleek, Art Deco-inspired lines and lavish interiors, the ship quickly gained a reputation as the epitome of luxury, attracting the world's elite and earning the nickname "the Grey Ghost" for its graceful silhouette. Throughout the 1930s, the Queen Mary hosted luminaries such as the Duke and Duchess of Windsor, Clark Gable, and Winston Churchill, its glamour and sophistication rivalling that of the finest hotels and restaurants in Europe and America.

As World War II erupted, the Queen Mary's role took a dramatic turn, as the British government requisitioned the ship for use as a troop transport. Its speed and capacity made it an invaluable asset in the war effort, carrying thousands of soldiers and vital supplies across the Atlantic while evading the deadly U-boats that prowled the depths. During this time, the ship's opulent furnishings were stripped away, its staterooms and public spaces converted into cramped quarters for the men and women who served their country in the fight against tyranny.

Following the end of the war, the Queen Mary was refitted and returned to its original purpose as a luxury ocean liner, resuming its transatlantic crossings and regaining its status as a symbol of glamour and refinement. However, the rise of commercial air travel in the 1950s and 1960s spelled the end of the golden age of ocean liners, as passengers increasingly opted for the speed and convenience of aeroplanes over the leisurely pace of life at sea. In 1967, after more than three decades of service, the Queen Mary was retired from active duty and found a permanent home in Long Beach, California, where it has been preserved as a floating hotel, museum, and testament to a bygone era.

It is within the hallowed halls of this historic vessel that countless tales of ghostly encounters have emerged, as visitors and staff alike report strange happenings and unexplained phenomena that defy rational explanation. The stories range from the eerie to the outright chilling, with reports of disembodied voices, cold spots, and spectral apparitions that seem to defy the laws of physics.

One of the most famous ghostly residents of the Queen Mary is said to be the spirit of a young girl named Jackie, who is believed to have drowned in the ship's first-class swimming pool during the 1930s or 1940s. Her laughter and playful splashing are frequently heard by visitors and staff, and her apparition has been seen on numerous occasions, often accompanied by the scent of flowers or the sound of distant music.

Another well-known spectral figure is that of a man named John Pedder, a fireman who tragically lost his life in the ship's engine room in 1966 when he was crushed by a watertight door during a routine drill. His ghost is said to roam the corridors and passageways near the site of the accident, leaving behind greasy handprints and occasionally appearing as a shadowy figure to unsuspecting visitors. Some have even claimed to feel an inexplicable sense of sadness or dread in the area where Pedder met his untimely end.

The Queen's Salon, once a luxurious gathering place for the ship's elite passengers, is another hotspot for paranormal activity. Here, the spirit of a beautiful woman in a flowing white gown has been seen dancing alone, her ethereal figure vanishing as quickly as it appears. Some believe her to be the ghost of a former passenger who met a tragic end aboard the ship, while others speculate that she may be a residual energy, forever replaying a moment from the Queen Mary's glamorous past.

The ship's infirmary and isolation ward, where sick and injured passengers were treated during the ship's heyday, is another area where paranormal activity has been reported. Visitors have described feeling sudden temperature drops, hearing disembodied voices, and even witnessing the apparition of a doctor or nurse dressed in period clothing. These ghostly medical personnel seem to be going about their duties, tending to patients who are no longer there, a testament to the dedication and professionalism that characterised the Queen Mary's crew.

While the stories of the Queen Mary's ghostly inhabitants may be spine-chilling, they also serve to illuminate the rich tapestry of human experience that unfolded within the ship's storied walls. Each spectral encounter, whether it be the laughter of a young girl who met a tragic end or the solemn visage of a fallen crew member, offers a glimpse into the lives of those who once called the ship home.

As a living museum and testament to a bygone era, the Queen Mary offers a unique opportunity to explore the fascinating intersection of history, human emotion, and the supernatural. The ship's luxurious staterooms and elegant public spaces, once the domain of the rich and famous, now provide a stage for the ghostly manifestations that have captured the imaginations of generations of visitors.

What is it about the Queen Mary that seems to attract such a wealth of paranormal activity? Some speculate that the ship's long and varied history, spanning the heights of luxury and the depths of human conflict, has imbued it with an energy that is both captivating and unsettling. Others believe that the ship's sheer size and complexity create an environment ripe for the manifestation of ghostly phenomena, as the many layers of history and emotion intertwine and overlap within its grand confines.

Regardless of the explanation, the Queen Mary's haunted reputation continues to draw visitors from around the world, eager to experience the thrill of the unknown and explore the ship's storied past. Whether one is a believer in the paranormal or simply a curious observer, the tales of ghostly encounters and eerie happenings that permeate the ship's history offer a unique and captivating glimpse into a world beyond our own.

As we journey through the haunted waters of history's most enigmatic vessels, the Queen Mary stands as a testament to the power of the human spirit and the enduring fascination with the supernatural. From its illustrious beginnings as a symbol of luxury and refinement to its current incarnation as a haunted attraction, the ship's ghostly residents serve as a reminder of the countless lives that have intersected within its walls, their stories forever etched into the fabric of this magnificent vessel. And as the sun sets over the Long Beach harbour and the shadows lengthen across the ship's deck, one cannot help but wonder what other secrets lie hidden within the Queen Mary, waiting to be discovered by those who dare to venture into the realm of the unknown.

The USS Hornet: The Haunted Aircraft Carrier

The USS Hornet, a storied aircraft carrier with a dark past, casts an imposing shadow over the waters of San Francisco Bay. This historic warship, now a floating museum, has seen its fair share of death, tragedy, and valour, serving as the stage for countless human dramas that unfolded on its decks during the turbulence of World War II and the Vietnam War. It is perhaps no wonder, then, that the spirits of those who served aboard the Hornet seem to linger within its cavernous hangars and narrow passageways, the echoes of their lives forever imprinted on the fabric of this mighty vessel.

Commissioned in 1943, the USS Hornet (CV-12) was the eighth ship to bear the name and quickly proved itself to be a formidable force in the Pacific theatre. Over the course of the war, the Hornet participated in numerous critical battles, including the Marianas Turkey Shoot, the Battle of Leyte Gulf, and the Battle of Okinawa. Its crew fought valiantly, earning the ship nine battle stars and a reputation for tenacity and courage.

Following the end of World War II, the Hornet was modernised and continued to serve in the Korean War and the Vietnam War, as well as participating in the recovery of the Apollo 11 and Apollo 12 astronauts. Finally, in 1970, the ship was decommissioned and left to rust in a naval shipyard, destined to be scrapped. However, a dedicated group of volunteers saved the Hornet from the scrapyard and transformed it into a floating museum, ensuring that its legacy would live on for future generations to learn from and appreciate.

With such a storied past, it is hardly surprising that the USS Hornet has gained a reputation as one of the most haunted ships in the United States. Over the years, visitors and staff alike have reported numerous unexplained phenomena and ghostly encounters, from eerie whispers and sudden cold spots to apparitions of long-dead sailors still going about their duties.

One of the most famous spirits said to haunt the Hornet is that of a young sailor known as "The Dress Whites Ghost." This apparition has been seen on numerous occasions in the ship's lower decks, dressed in the crisp white uniform that was once the standard attire for naval personnel. Some witnesses have reported seeing the figure walking silently through the corridors, while others claim to have spotted him standing at attention near the ship's barber shop, as if awaiting a long-overdue haircut.

Another ghostly resident of the Hornet is the spirit of a man who appears in the vicinity of the ship's sickbay, where the injured and ailing crew members were treated during the vessel's years of active service. The apparition is often described as a tall, gaunt figure with hollow eyes and an expression of profound sadness. Some speculate that this spirit may be that of a medical officer who served aboard the ship and was unable to save the lives of his comrades, while others believe that he may be a former patient who succumbed to his injuries.

One particularly chilling account comes from a former volunteer who claims to have encountered a ghostly sailor in one of the ship's many cramped sleeping quarters. The volunteer was working alone, cleaning and restoring the bunks, when he suddenly felt a hand on his shoulder and heard a voice whisper in his ear, urging him to leave the room. When he turned to confront the intruder, he found himself face-to-face with the transparent figure of a sailor, his eyes filled with a mixture of sadness and urgency. The volunteer quickly left the room, shaken by the encounter and unable to explain what he had just experienced.

In addition to the spirits of the sailors who served aboard the Hornet, the ship also seems to be home to several other ghostly entities, each with their own unique stories and connections to the vessel. One such spirit is that of a young Japanese pilot who is believed to have perished during an attack on the aircraft carrier. Witnesses have reported seeing the apparition, dressed in the flight gear of the Imperial Japanese Navy, wandering the ship's hangars and flight deck, seemingly lost and disoriented.

Another eerie presence aboard the Hornet is that of a mysterious black cat, which has been seen by multiple visitors and staff members over the years. This spectral feline is often spotted lurking in the ship's darkest corners or darting silently through the narrow passageways, only to vanish as suddenly as it appeared. Some believe that the ghostly cat may be a manifestation of the many pets and mascots that served as companions and sources of comfort for the sailors during their long and perilous deployments.

As the stories of the USS Hornet's ghostly inhabitants continue to circulate, paranormal enthusiasts and history buffs alike are drawn to the ship, eager to explore its haunted decks and uncover the secrets that lie hidden within its rusting hull. Guided tours of the vessel offer a unique opportunity to delve into the ship's storied past while keeping an eye out for signs of the supernatural, from unexplained footsteps and disembodied voices to the fleeting glimpses of spectral figures that are said to linger in the shadows.

What is it about the USS Hornet that seems to attract such a wealth of paranormal activity? Some suggest that the ship's long history of war and human suffering has left an indelible mark on the vessel, creating an environment ripe for ghostly manifestations. Others point to the ship's status as a floating museum, where the memories and emotions of those who served aboard the Hornet are preserved and honoured, providing a fertile ground for spiritual energy to manifest.

Regardless of the reasons behind the Hornet's haunted reputation, it is clear that the ship offers a unique and captivating glimpse into the world of the supernatural. As a testament to the courage and sacrifice of the men who served aboard this historic warship, the spirits of the USS Hornet continue to captivate the imaginations of those who dare to venture within its rusting confines.

As we continue our journey through the haunted waters of history's most enigmatic vessels, the USS Hornet stands as a poignant reminder of the human cost of war and the enduring strength of the human spirit. From the spectral sailors who still seem to carry out their duties to the ghostly apparitions of fallen foes, the Hornet's haunted decks offer a fascinating window into the world beyond our own, where the echoes of the past continue to resonate and the spirits of the departed linger just beyond the veil of our perception.

As the sun sets over San Francisco Bay and the shadows lengthen across the ship's imposing silhouette, one cannot help but wonder what other secrets lie hidden within the USS Hornet, waiting to be discovered by those brave enough to delve into the mysteries of the unknown. Will you be among those who dare to explore the haunted depths of this historic warship and uncover the chilling secrets that lie beneath its weathered exterior? Only time will tell, as the USS Hornet continues to sail the haunted waters of history, its ghostly inhabitants forever bound to the vessel that was once their home.

The Mary Celeste: The Ultimate Maritime Mystery

The story of the Mary Celeste is one that has captivated the imaginations of countless generations, becoming synonymous with the very idea of maritime mystery. The eerie events surrounding the abandonment of this seemingly unremarkable merchant brigantine have sparked endless speculation and debate, giving rise to a plethora of ghostly legends that persist to this day. In this enthralling chapter, we will delve into the fascinating history of the Mary Celeste and investigate the strange circumstances that transformed her into the ultimate symbol of nautical enigma.

The Mary Celeste was built in 1860 in Spencer's Island, Nova Scotia, and was originally named the Amazon. Over the course of her early years, the ship would change hands and names several times, eventually being purchased by a group of American investors in 1868, who renamed her the Mary Celeste. Despite her tumultuous beginnings, the ship was a fine example of a mid-19th-century merchant vessel, designed for speed and durability as she plied the trade routes of the Atlantic.

The fateful voyage that would forever seal the Mary Celeste's place in history began on November 7, 1872. The ship set sail from New York City bound for Genoa, Italy, carrying a cargo of 1,701 barrels of industrial alcohol. The ship's experienced captain, Benjamin Briggs, was accompanied by his wife, Sarah, their two-year-old daughter, Sophia, and a crew of seven men, all of whom were considered reliable and trustworthy sailors.

Less than a month into the voyage, on December 5, 1872, the Mary Celeste would be discovered adrift and abandoned by the crew of the British brigantine Dei Gratia. The circumstances surrounding the discovery were as baffling as they were eerie: the Mary Celeste was found to be in good seaworthy condition, with no signs of damage or struggle, and her cargo was largely intact. The ship's lifeboat was missing, along with its captain, his family, and the entire crew, who had seemingly vanished without a trace.

The mystery deepened as the crew of the Dei Gratia investigated the abandoned vessel. The Mary Celeste's logbook revealed no clues as to the fate of her missing occupants, and the ship's provisions and personal belongings were found to be undisturbed. The only signs of anything amiss were a few feet of water in the hold and the ship's chronometer and sextant missing from the captain's cabin. With no evidence of piracy, mutiny, or any other clear explanation for the disappearance, the crew of the Dei Gratia took charge of the Mary Celeste and sailed her to Gibraltar, where an exhaustive salvage inquiry would attempt to unravel the enigmatic events that had befallen the doomed vessel.

As word of the Mary Celeste's eerie discovery spread, the ship's story quickly became the stuff of legend, capturing the imaginations of people around the world. Theories and conjectures abounded, each more outlandish than the last: some suggested that a sudden waterspout had swept the crew overboard, while others speculated that the ship's cargo of alcohol had leaked and exploded, forcing the captain and crew to abandon ship in a panic. Still, others posited that supernatural forces were at play, with whispers of ghostly apparitions and cursed artefacts fueling the fires of speculation.

Despite the exhaustive efforts of the salvage inquiry, the fate of the Mary Celeste's captain, his family, and the crew would remain an unsolved mystery, leaving the ship with a dark and haunted legacy that persists to this day. Over the years, countless retellings and embellishments of the Mary Celeste's tale have added to the ship's mystique, transforming her into a vessel of myth and legend, a symbol of the unexplainable and the unknown that lurks within the depths of the ocean.

As the legend of the Mary Celeste continued to grow, so too did the ghostly tales associated with the ship. Seafarers who came into contact with the vessel after her fateful voyage spoke of strange occurrences and eerie sensations, as if the spirits of the missing captain, his family, and the crew still lingered on board, forever trapped within the confines of the ship. Some claimed to have witnessed phantom figures on deck or heard disembodied voices echoing through the empty spaces below. Others reported feeling an overwhelming sense of dread, as though some malevolent force was watching them from the shadows.

But the ghostly legends of the Mary Celeste are not limited to the ship itself. Over the years, many have claimed to have encountered the apparition of Captain Benjamin Briggs, who is said to haunt the waters where his ship was found adrift. These spectral sightings often describe a figure standing at the helm of a ghostly vessel, his face etched with anguish and despair as he searches in vain for his missing family and crew. Some believe that his spirit is doomed to roam the sea for eternity, unable to find peace until the truth of the Mary Celeste's fate is finally revealed.

Another chilling aspect of the Mary Celeste's legend is the so-called "Mary Celeste Curse." This alleged curse is said to have befallen those who came into possession of items taken from the ship, with numerous accounts of misfortune and tragedy befalling those who dared to claim a piece of the haunted vessel for themselves. Tales of unexplained accidents, sudden illnesses, and even deaths have been attributed to the curse, adding yet another layer of intrigue to the ship's already enigmatic history.

Despite the countless theories and investigations into the Mary Celeste's fate, the truth of what transpired during that fateful voyage in 1872 remains shrouded in mystery. The ship herself would continue to sail the seas for over a decade after her eerie discovery, her haunted reputation casting a shadow over her every voyage. Eventually, the Mary Celeste would meet her end in 1885, deliberately wrecked off the coast of Haiti in an ill-fated attempt at insurance fraud.

The enduring fascination with the Mary Celeste speaks to the deep-rooted human desire to understand the unknown and to seek answers to the unexplained. Her story has become a testament to the power of imagination and the allure of the supernatural, capturing the hearts and minds of generations of readers, historians, and paranormal enthusiasts alike. The ghostly legends and eerie mysteries that surround the Mary Celeste ensure that her name will forever be synonymous with maritime enigma, a haunting reminder of the secrets that still lie hidden beneath the waves.

And so, as we close this chapter on the Mary Celeste, we are left with more questions than answers, our imaginations stirred by the haunting tales and eerie legends that have grown around this ill-fated ship. As we continue our journey through the haunted waters of history's most enigmatic vessels, we are reminded that the sea is a place of mystery and wonder, where the line between the natural and the supernatural is often blurred.

The Star of India: A Haunting Voyage

Steeped in history and adorned with the scars of countless voyages across the world's most treacherous waters, the Star of India stands as a testament to the golden age of sail. Launched in 1863, this iron-hulled sailing ship has seen her fair share of storms, mutinies, and hardships, but she has also been witness to a darker, more ethereal side of maritime lore – the world of hauntings and paranormal encounters.

The Star of India's story began on the Isle of Man, where she was built by Gibson, McDonald & Arnold for the merchant firm J. P. Corry & Company. Initially christened Euterpe, after the Greek muse of music, she embarked on her maiden voyage on December 6, 1863, from Liverpool, England, to Calcutta, India. It was the first of many journeys she would undertake in the service of global trade, traversing the treacherous Cape Horn on more than twenty occasions, and circumnavigating the globe over two dozen times.

Throughout her long and storied career, the Star of India would be tested by the elements and the whims of fate. She endured countless storms, collisions, and groundings, and even survived a mutiny during her time as a British immigrant ship. Despite the many hardships she faced, the ship remained steadfast and resolute, earning her place in history as one of the world's oldest active sailing ships.

In 1926, after years of devoted service, the Star of India was sold to the Zoological Society of San Diego for the sum of $9,000. She was brought to the city's harbour and transformed into a floating museum, preserving her legacy for future generations to appreciate and admire. But as visitors began to explore the ship's storied decks and narrow passageways, it became clear that the Star of India was more than just a relic of a bygone era – she was a vessel teeming with restless spirits and haunted by the memories of her storied past.

One of the most famous ghostly residents of the Star of India is the spirit of a young stowaway, believed to have hidden aboard the ship during one of her early voyages. The boy, thought to be around seventeen years old, was discovered by the crew and put to work in the ship's galley. However, his time aboard the Star of India would be short-lived, as he would tragically lose his life in a fall from the ship's rigging.

The spirit of the young stowaway is said to roam the decks and passageways of the Star of India, his presence often heralded by the sound of footsteps echoing through the ship's empty spaces. Visitors and crew members alike have reported encounters with the boy's apparition, describing him as a shy, sombre figure dressed in period clothing, who vanishes as quickly as he appears. Some believe that his spirit remains trapped aboard the ship, forever bound to the vessel that became both his refuge and his tomb.

Another spectral presence that haunts the Star of India is that of Captain S. A. Lofthouse, who served as the ship's master during the early 20th century. A stern and disciplined man, Captain Lofthouse was known for his unyielding devotion to duty and his commitment to maintaining order among his crew. It is said that his spirit continues to watch over the ship, ensuring that her visitors and caretakers treat her with the respect and reverence she deserves.

Captain Lofthouse's ghost has been seen in various parts of the

Star of India, most notably in his former quarters and on the ship's deck. His apparition is often described as a tall, imposing figure dressed in a captain's uniform, with an air of authority and a piercing gaze. Many who have encountered Captain Lofthouse's spirit report feeling a sense of awe and respect, as if they are in the presence of a powerful force that demands obedience.

In addition to the spirits of the young stowaway and Captain Lofthouse, the Star of India is said to be haunted by the ghost of a crew member who met his untimely demise in the ship's anchor chain locker. The man, whose identity remains unknown, was crushed to death during a tragic accident when the anchor chain was released. His restless spirit is said to haunt the area where he perished, with visitors and staff alike reporting strange noises, unexplained cold spots, and a palpable sense of unease emanating from the chain locker.

Perhaps the most chilling account of a paranormal encounter aboard the Star of India comes from a former caretaker of the ship, who shared his experience during an interview with a local news station. The man, who asked to remain anonymous, spoke of a night when he was working alone on the ship, performing routine maintenance tasks. As he made his way through the dark and silent passageways, he suddenly became aware of a presence behind him – the unmistakable sensation of being watched.

The caretaker turned to confront his unseen pursuer, only to find himself face to face with the ghostly figure of a man dressed in period clothing, his eyes locked in a gaze that seemed to bore into the caretaker's very soul. The apparition stood motionless, its presence filling the narrow corridor with an overwhelming sense of dread. Then, just as suddenly as it had appeared, the ghostly figure vanished into thin air, leaving the caretaker shaken and forever changed by his encounter with the unknown.

The Star of India's haunted reputation has attracted paranormal enthusiasts and investigators from all corners of the globe, each seeking to uncover the truth behind the ship's many ghostly tales. Some have come away with tantalising evidence of supernatural activity – EVP recordings, unexplained temperature fluctuations, and even photographs of shadowy figures lurking in the ship's darkest corners. Others have left with only their own personal experiences to ponder, the memories of eerie encounters and spine-tingling sensations forever etched in their minds.

As the Star of India continues to cast her spell over visitors and ghost hunters alike, one thing remains clear – this storied ship is more than just a monument to the past; she is a vessel that carries with her the weight of countless souls, their stories forever intertwined with her iron hull and weathered decks. For those who dare to step aboard and explore her haunted spaces, the Star of India offers a glimpse into a world where the boundaries between the living and the dead are blurred, and the mysteries of the past come alive in the most unexpected of ways.

The HMS Victory: Naval Battles and Restless Spirits

The HMS Victory stands as a symbol of British naval prowess and a testament to the courage and determination of those who served within her wooden hull. Launched in 1765, this first-rate ship of the line has played a pivotal role in some of the most significant naval battles in history, including the infamous Battle of Trafalgar, where Admiral Lord Nelson met his untimely demise. Yet, as one delves deeper into the storied past of this remarkable vessel, it becomes apparent that the HMS Victory is not only a relic of maritime history, but also a hotbed of paranormal activity and ghostly encounters.

To truly understand the haunted history of the HMS Victory, one must first appreciate the vessel's impressive military record. With 104 guns and a crew of over 800 men, the Victory was a formidable force on the high seas, capable of striking fear into the hearts of her enemies. Her most famous engagement, the

Battle of Trafalgar, took place on October 21, 1805, and saw the British fleet, under the command of Admiral Nelson, decisively defeat a combined French and Spanish force. It was during this battle that Nelson, the hero of the British Navy, was fatally wounded by a French sniper, his death marking the end of an illustrious career and the beginning of his ship's haunted legacy.

Admiral Nelson's spirit is said to be among the restless souls that still inhabit the HMS Victory, his ghostly presence often reported in the vicinity of the ship's quarterdeck, where he fell during the Battle of Trafalgar. Visitors and crew members alike have described encountering a spectral figure dressed in a naval officer's uniform, complete with the distinctive decorations and medals that adorned Nelson's person. These encounters are often accompanied by the scent of Nelson's favourite fragrance, a blend of bay leaves and sandalwood, which fills the air around the apparition before it disappears from sight.

The spirit of Admiral Nelson is not the only ghostly inhabitant of the HMS Victory. Another well-known spectre is that of a young sailor named Fred, who is said to have perished in a tragic accident aboard the ship. Fred's spirit is known for his mischievous nature, as he often makes his presence known by moving objects, creating unexplained noises, and even tugging at the clothing of unsuspecting visitors. While his antics are generally regarded as harmless, they serve as a constant reminder of the young lives that were forever altered by the harsh realities of naval service.

Perhaps the most chilling paranormal encounter reported aboard the HMS Victory is the experience of a former caretaker who spent a night locked inside the ship as part of a charity event. As the man explored the dark, silent passageways, he became aware of a presence that seemed to be following him, the sound of footsteps echoing through the ship's empty corridors. The caretaker turned to confront his unseen pursuer, only to be met with the sight of a ghostly figure dressed in the tattered remains of a naval uniform. The apparition stared at the caretaker with hollow, lifeless eyes before vanishing into the darkness, leaving the man with a haunting memory that would stay with him for the rest of his days.

The paranormal activity aboard the HMS Victory is not limited to apparitions and unexplained noises. Many visitors to the ship have reported experiencing sudden drops in temperature, cold spots that seem to defy explanation, and the overwhelming sensation of being watched by unseen eyes. Some have even claimed to hear the distant sounds of battle, the clash of swords and the roar of cannon fire, as if the ship's storied past is still playing out within her wooden hull.

As one explores the haunted halls of the HMS Victory, it becomes increasingly apparent that the spirits of those who served and perished aboard this historic vessel are still very much a part of her legacy. Their presence, whether manifested through apparitions, unexplained phenomena, or fleeting sensations, serves as a testament to the powerful bond that exists between the ship and her crew, a connection that transcends the boundaries of time and mortality.

The haunted history of the HMS Victory is not only a source of fascination for paranormal enthusiasts, but also a poignant reminder of the sacrifices made by the men who served within her wooden hull. The countless souls who lost their lives in the pursuit of victory, both in battle and through the daily perils of naval life, continue to leave their mark on the ship that was their home and their final resting place. As visitors to the HMS Victory delve into her past and explore her ghostly tales, they are also honouring the memory of these brave men, who fought and died for their country and their comrades.

One particularly evocative tale of supernatural activity aboard the HMS Victory concerns a group of tourists who were exploring the ship's lower decks during a guided tour. As they made their way through the dimly lit passageways, one woman in the group suddenly felt a firm hand on her shoulder, as if someone was trying to get her attention. She turned to see who it was, only to find herself face to face with the ghostly figure of a young sailor, his eyes filled with a desperate urgency. The apparition held her gaze for a brief moment before vanishing into the shadows, leaving the woman and her fellow tourists stunned and shaken by the encounter.

This and other accounts of ghostly encounters aboard the HMS Victory have attracted the attention of paranormal investigators, who have descended upon the ship in search of definitive evidence of supernatural activity. Some have come away with tantalising clues, such as EVP recordings and unexplained temperature fluctuations, while others have left with only their own experiences and impressions to guide them. Yet, as the ship's haunted legacy continues to captivate and intrigue, one thing remains certain – the spirits of the HMS Victory are far from silent, their voices echoing through the centuries in a chorus of eternal devotion.

The Octavius: Frozen Ghost Ship of the Arctic

There are few tales more chilling and evocative than the legend of the Octavius, a lost vessel discovered adrift in the icy waters of the Arctic, her frozen crew still on board. This haunting story has captivated the imaginations of seafarers and paranormal enthusiasts alike for centuries, serving as a stark reminder of the perilous nature of maritime exploration and the mysterious forces that sometimes conspire to doom those who venture into the unknown.

The Octavius began her fateful journey in 1761, setting sail from London bound for the Orient. Laden with a valuable cargo of trade goods, the ship was captained by a man eager to make his mark in the world of maritime commerce. The voyage was relatively uneventful, and the Octavius reached her destination without incident, her crew enjoying the exotic sights and sounds of the Far East before preparing for their return journey to

England.

It was at this point that the ship's captain made a fateful decision, one that would ultimately seal the fate of both his vessel and his crew. Hoping to shave valuable time off their return voyage, he chose to attempt a shortcut through the treacherous waters of the Arctic, a route that few had dared to navigate and even fewer had successfully traversed. Undaunted by the risks, the captain charted a course that would take the Octavius through the ice-choked seas of the Northwest Passage, a decision that would ultimately prove to be his undoing.

As the Octavius ventured deeper into the icy realm of the Arctic, her crew found themselves confronted with a world of unparalleled beauty and danger. Towering icebergs loomed on the horizon, their shimmering surfaces glinting in the weak rays of the midnight sun, while the ship's wooden hull groaned and creaked in protest as it fought its way through the encroaching ice. Despite the increasingly perilous conditions, the captain pressed on, his determination to succeed driving him and his crew ever closer to the edge of disaster.

It is impossible to say for certain what fate ultimately befell the Octavius, as the ship and her crew seemingly vanished without a trace, swallowed up by the icy embrace of the Arctic. Yet, the story of this ill-fated vessel does not end there, for it is said that the Octavius was discovered adrift in the frozen waters of the Arctic some 13 years later, her crew still on board and encased in ice, a ghostly testament to the power of nature and the folly of human ambition.

The chilling tale of the Octavius' discovery is said to have been passed down by the crew of the whaling vessel Herald, who stumbled upon the ghostly ship in the waters off the coast of Greenland in 1775. As the Herald drew closer to the derelict vessel, the whalers could scarcely believe their eyes, for the Octavius appeared to be frozen in time, her masts and rigging encased in a thick layer of ice, and her once-proud figurehead now a grotesque, frost-covered spectre.

Boarding the Octavius, the crew of the Herald found themselves confronted with a scene of unimaginable horror. The ship's occupants lay where they had fallen, their bodies preserved in the icy tomb that had once been their home. The captain was discovered seated at his desk, his pen still in hand, a look of grim determination etched upon his frozen features. The ship's log, which lay open before him, revealed that the Octavius had indeed attempted to navigate the treacherous waters of the

Northwest Passage, only to become hopelessly trapped in the ice, her crew doomed to a slow and agonising death as the unforgiving Arctic claimed them one by one.

Further exploration of the ship revealed more harrowing scenes. Huddled together in a desperate attempt to stave off the bitter cold, the frozen forms of the crewmen seemed to bear silent witness to the horrors they had endured. In the dim, frost-encrusted confines of the hold, the once-valuable cargo lay untouched, a haunting reminder of the dreams and ambitions that had driven these men to their doom.

As the crew of the Herald attempted to come to terms with the ghastly spectacle before them, they could not help but feel a growing sense of unease, as if the very air around them was charged with the lingering anguish and despair of the Octavius' lost souls. Reluctantly, the whalers decided to leave the ship and her frozen occupants to their eternal rest, the eerie image of the Octavius and her tragic crew forever etched in their memories.

The tale of the Octavius has since become the stuff of legend, a chilling reminder of the dangers that await those who venture into the uncharted realms of the earth. Whether fact or fiction, the story serves as a stark warning of the power of nature to humble even the most determined and intrepid of souls, as well as a haunting testament to the indomitable spirit of those who dare to defy the odds in the pursuit of fortune and glory.

Yet, the legend of the Octavius does not end with her discovery by the crew of the Herald. Over the years, there have been numerous reports of a ghostly ship, her icy masts and frost-covered figurehead gliding silently through the fog-shrouded waters of the Arctic. Sailors who claim to have encountered this spectral vessel speak of an overwhelming sense of dread and despair, as if the very air around them is charged with the lingering echoes of the Octavius' tragic fate.

These ghostly sightings have fueled speculation that the Octavius is more than just a cautionary tale, but rather a vessel doomed to roam the icy waters of the Arctic for all eternity, her frozen crew forever trapped in the icy grip of the sea. While sceptics may dismiss these accounts as mere sailor's yarns, those who have experienced the chilling presence of the Octavius firsthand are often left with little doubt that the ship and her tragic occupants are still very much a part of the world of the living, their restless spirits destined to haunt the waters of the Arctic until the end of time.

The legend of the Octavius serves as a poignant reminder of the power of the sea to inspire both awe and terror, and the fascination that tales of haunted ships and ghostly encounters continue to hold for those who dare to venture into the realm of the unknown. As the sun sets and the icy waters of the Arctic are cloaked in darkness, one cannot help but ponder the mysteries that lie hidden beneath the waves, and the ghostly apparitions that are said to haunt the deep.

As we leave the chilling tale of the Octavius and her frozen crew behind, we are reminded of the power of the paranormal to captivate and intrigue the imagination, and the enduring fascination that tales of haunted ships and supernatural encounters at sea continue to hold for those who are drawn to the world of the unexplained. The Octavius, whether real or imagined, serves as a haunting testament to the power of the human spirit to endure in the face of unimaginable adversity, and the timeless allure of the mysteries that lie hidden beneath the surface of the sea.

And so, our exploration of the haunted realm of the Octavius comes to an end, leaving us with a renewed appreciation for the chilling tales and ghostly encounters that continue to enthral and captivate the imagination.

The Lady Lovibond: The Ghost Ship of Goodwin Sands

The waters of the English Channel have long been the scene of countless maritime tragedies, the deadly embrace of its treacherous currents and unforgiving weather claiming the lives of sailors and passengers alike. Among the many shipwrecks that litter the seabed, few stories are as haunting and tragic as that of the Lady Lovibond, a vessel whose chilling legacy has transcended the centuries to become one of the most enduring legends of the sea. In this chapter, we will delve into the tragic tale of the Lady Lovibond and its phantom vessel that continues to haunt the treacherous Goodwin Sands, a story steeped in passion, betrayal, and the restless spirits of those who lost their lives on that fateful night so long ago.

Our tale begins in the early 18th century, as the Lady Lovibond, a beautifully crafted three-masted schooner, prepared to set sail from London on a voyage to Portugal. The ship was captained by the dashing Simon Reed, a seasoned seafarer who was well-versed in the ways of the ocean. The journey was to be a momentous one for Reed, as he had recently married his beloved Annetta, and the couple had decided to celebrate their nuptials by embarking on a romantic voyage together, accompanied by a small but capable crew.

Little did the newlyweds know that their joy would be short-lived, for among the crew was John Rivers, the ship's first mate and a man who harboured a secret, all-consuming passion for the beautiful Annetta. As the Lady Lovibond made her way down the Thames and into the English Channel, Rivers' jealousy and bitterness began to fester, slowly consuming him as he watched his beloved in the arms of another man.

As the ship approached the treacherous waters of the Goodwin Sands, a notorious sandbank known for its deadly currents and ever-shifting sands, Rivers made a decision that would seal the fate of all on board. In a fit of blind rage and despair, he took advantage of the darkness and confusion of a stormy night to seize control of the ship, steering her straight into the heart of the deadly sands.

The Lady Lovibond met her end on the night of February 13,

1748, her hull impaled upon the jagged sands as the merciless waves battered her mercilessly until she was finally swallowed by the sea. All on board perished in the icy embrace of the Channel, their lives snuffed out in an instant by Rivers' vengeful hand.

But the story of the Lady Lovibond does not end with her tragic demise. For centuries, sailors navigating the treacherous waters of the English Channel have reported sightings of a ghostly ship, her ethereal masts and spectral sails gliding silently across the waves, her crew seemingly unaware of their own demise as they go about their duties with grim determination. This phantom vessel, it is said, is none other than the Lady Lovibond herself, her restless spirit forever doomed to haunt the scene of her tragic end.

These ghostly sightings have occurred with eerie regularity, often on the very anniversary of the ship's fateful wreck. Over the years, countless mariners have reported encountering the spectral Lady Lovibond, her ghostly form emerging from the mist and fog to send shivers down the spines of even the most seasoned sailors. Some have claimed to hear the anguished cries of her doomed crew, their voices carried on the wind like the whispers of the damned, while others have reported a sudden, inexplicable chill in the air, as if the very sea itself were mourning the lost souls of the Lady Lovibond.

The legend of the Lady Lovibond has captivated the imaginations of countless people throughout the centuries, and the story has become an enduring part of English maritime folklore. Some have speculated that the ship's tragic fate was the result of a curse, a supernatural punishment for the jealousy and betrayal that had been allowed to fester within the hearts of its crew. Others maintain that the restless spirits of the Lady Lovibond's crew are simply unable to move on from the scene of their tragic demise, forever trapped in a limbo between life and death, their phantom ship a chilling reminder of the terrible price of unbridled passion and vengeance.

The Goodwin Sands, where the Lady Lovibond met her tragic end, have long been a source of fascination and fear for those who ply the waters of the English Channel. Over the years, these treacherous sands have claimed the lives of countless sailors and have become the final resting place of more than 2,000 shipwrecks. The shifting sands of the Goodwins have concealed these watery graves from the prying eyes of the living, leaving the stories of the doomed vessels and their unfortunate crews to be whispered among the sailors who brave these perilous waters.

Despite the countless tragedies that have occurred within the Goodwin Sands, the haunting tale of the Lady Lovibond remains one of the most enduring and chilling. The story has been passed down through the generations, a cautionary tale of the perils of unchecked jealousy and the supernatural forces that are said to lurk beneath the waves, waiting to claim the unwary.

As the years have passed, the legend of the Lady Lovibond has continued to capture the imagination of those who hear it, inspiring countless stories, poems, and works of art that seek to explore the enigmatic mystery of this ghostly ship and its tragic crew. The tale has become a potent symbol of the power of love, loss, and betrayal to haunt the human heart, and a chilling reminder of the supernatural forces that some believe still hold sway over the world's oceans.

The haunting tale of the Lady Lovibond is just one of many chilling stories that have emerged from the depths of maritime history, but its enduring legacy serves as a testament to the power of such tales to captivate and terrify in equal measure. As long as there are ships and sailors to navigate the world's oceans, there will be ghostly vessels and eerie phenomena to haunt their waking dreams, a reminder of the mysteries that still lurk beneath the surface of the deep blue sea.

In the years since the tragic demise of the Lady Lovibond, the legend has continued to evolve and grow, as each new generation of sailors adds their own stories and experiences to the rich tapestry of maritime lore. Whether viewed as a chilling ghost story or a cautionary tale of love and betrayal, the story of the Lady Lovibond and her phantom crew remains one of the most captivating and enduring legends of the sea, a chilling reminder of the power of the supernatural to both fascinate and horrify.

As we continue to explore the haunted waters of history's most enigmatic vessels, we are reminded of the deep connection between the sea and the supernatural, a bond that has captivated the human imagination for centuries. From the depths of the Bermuda Triangle to the ghostly apparitions of doomed steamboats, the world's oceans are a treasure trove of mystery and wonder, a realm where the boundaries between the natural and the supernatural grow thin and the unknown beckons to those who dare to venture beyond the horizon.

The SS Valencia: The Graveyard of the Pacific's Haunted Wreck

The Pacific Northwest, with its rugged coastlines, treacherous waters, and tumultuous weather, has long been known as the "Graveyard of the Pacific." Over the centuries, many ships have met their doom in these perilous waters. However, few stories are as haunting as that of the SS Valencia, an ill-fated steamer whose tragic sinking and ghostly sightings of lifeboats continue to send chills down the spines of those who dare to venture into these foreboding seas.

Built in 1882 by William Cramp and Sons, a prominent shipbuilding company based in Philadelphia, the SS Valencia was a 1,598-ton iron-hulled passenger steamer. Commissioned by the Red D Line, she was intended for service between Venezuela and New York City. The vessel featured state-of-the-art technology of its time, including electric lights and a refrigeration system. For the first decade of her existence, the Valencia led an uneventful life, making routine trips between her intended ports of call.

In 1897, the Valencia was purchased by the Pacific Coast Steamship Company and transferred to the West Coast, where she began service between San Francisco and Seattle. However, by the turn of the century, the once-proud steamer had begun to show her age, and in 1905, she was relegated to serving as a reserve vessel for the company's fleet.

The Valencia's final voyage began on January 20, 1906, when she set sail from San Francisco bound for Victoria and Vancouver, British Columbia, carrying 108 passengers and 65 crew members. The voyage was plagued by bad luck from the start, with the ship departing later than scheduled due to inclement weather. The late departure would ultimately seal the ship's fate.

As the Valencia steamed northward, a fierce storm blew in, battering the ship with gale-force winds and monstrous waves. Visibility was reduced to near zero, and the ship's captain, Thomas J. Johnson, was forced to rely on dead reckoning to navigate the treacherous waters. Unbeknownst to the captain and his crew, the ship was being pushed off course by the storm and strong currents.

In the early morning hours of January 22, the Valencia met her doom. The ship, having been pushed far off course, struck a reef near Pachena Point on the southwest coast of Vancouver Island. The impact tore a massive hole in the hull, and the ship quickly began taking on water. The crew scrambled to launch the lifeboats, but the stormy seas and the panicked passengers made the task nearly impossible.

Of the seven lifeboats on board, only three managed to make it away from the sinking ship. One capsized almost immediately, while another disappeared into the night, never to be seen again. The third lifeboat, carrying 18 survivors, managed to reach the shore. Meanwhile, the Valencia, her remaining passengers and crew still on board, was being relentlessly battered by the storm and the unforgiving reef. Those who remained aboard could do nothing but watch in horror as their ship was torn apart and slowly sank beneath the waves.

In the days following the tragedy, the beaches near the wreck were strewn with the bodies of the Valencia's passengers and crew. Of the 173 people who had set sail from San Francisco, only 37 survived. The loss of the Valencia was one of the worst maritime disasters in the history of the Pacific Northwest, and the tragic event would leave an indelible mark on the region.

The gruesome aftermath of the Valencia's sinking was only the beginning of the eerie tales that would come to surround the ship's wreck. Over the years, numerous reports of ghostly sightings and paranormal activity have emerged from the area where the Valencia met her tragic end. One of the most chilling of these tales involves the ghostly lifeboats that are said to haunt the waters near the site of the wreck.

Many mariners and local residents have reported seeing lifeboats, eerily similar in appearance to those of the SS Valencia, rowing silently through the fog-shrouded waters off the coast of Vancouver Island. These spectral vessels appear to be manned by ghostly figures, their faces etched with terror and despair as they row toward an unknown destination. The apparitions have been seen both day and night, and in various weather conditions, leaving those who witness them questioning the boundaries of reality.

These phantom lifeboats are not the only strange occurrences associated with the Valencia's wreck. Over the years, people have reported hearing the desperate cries of the ship's doomed passengers and crew echoing through the misty forests along the shoreline. These chilling sounds seem to be a haunting reminder of the harrowing night when the Valencia met her end, forever etched into the fabric of the place where so many lives were lost.

Divers who have ventured to the wreck site have also reported strange happenings. Some have claimed to feel an eerie presence, as if the souls of the Valencia's victims still linger in the watery depths. Others have reported hearing disembodied voices and phantom footsteps echoing through the wreck's twisted metal and rusted corridors. These ghostly manifestations seem to suggest that the spirits of the Valencia's passengers and crew are unable to find peace, still trapped in the twisted remains of their ill-fated vessel.

In addition to the ghostly sightings and eerie sounds, there have been numerous accounts of paranormal activity on the nearby shores. Residents and visitors alike have reported strange occurrences, such as unexplained cold spots, flickering lights, and the sensation of being watched by unseen eyes. These phenomena have only served to strengthen the belief that the tragic events of the Valencia's final voyage have left a permanent mark on the region, imbuing the area with an otherworldly energy that defies explanation.

The legend of the SS Valencia and her ghostly lifeboats has endured for more than a century, captivating the imaginations of those who hear the tale. The story serves as a poignant reminder of the power of the sea and the tragic consequences that can arise when human error and the forces of nature collide. As the decades pass, the haunting spectres of the Valencia's lifeboats continue to be seen in the waters off the coast of Vancouver Island, a chilling testament to one of the most tragic and mysterious maritime disasters in the history of the Pacific Northwest.

As you ponder the eerie tale of the SS Valencia and her phantom lifeboats, you may find yourself questioning the nature of the supernatural and the limits of human understanding. While some may dismiss these ghostly encounters as mere coincidence or the product of overactive imaginations, others are left to wonder if there is something more to these chilling stories, a hidden truth that lies just beyond our grasp.

The SS Valencia's haunting legacy serves as a powerful reminder of the countless lives that have been claimed by the unforgiving waters of the Graveyard of the Pacific. The ghostly manifestations that continue to be reported in the area are a testament to the enduring fascination and fear that surround these tragic events, and the power of the human spirit to persist, even in the face of unimaginable hardship and loss.

As you continue your journey through the pages of "Haunted Ships & Boats: Nautical Nightmares and Paranormal Encounters at Sea," allow the captivating and chilling tale of the SS Valencia to serve as a reminder of the enduring allure of the sea, its power to both create and destroy, and the haunting legacy that lingers in the wake of its darkest moments.

The Princess Augusta: The Palatine Light's Fiery Origins

The waters surrounding Block Island, a small isle located off the coast of Rhode Island, have long been known for their treacherous currents, sudden storms, and hidden shoals. These very waters are home to one of the most chilling maritime legends in American history, the haunting tale of the Princess Augusta, also known as the Palatine Light. The story of this ill-fated ship has been passed down through generations of sailors and islanders, inspiring shivers of terror and awe in those who dare to navigate the treacherous waters of the Atlantic Ocean.

In 1738, the Princess Augusta set sail from Rotterdam, the Netherlands, carrying a group of German Palatine immigrants seeking refuge and a better life in the American colonies. Among the passengers were men, women, and children, many of whom had sold their possessions to fund their passage across the treacherous Atlantic Ocean. Their dreams of a new life in the

New World, however, would soon be shattered by a series of tragic events that would result in the Princess Augusta becoming one of the most notorious ghost ships in history.

As the Princess Augusta embarked on its long and arduous journey, the ship was beset by numerous challenges, including storms, disease, and food shortages. Many of the passengers perished during the voyage, their bodies committed to the deep, while the survivors languished in their cramped and filthy quarters, suffering from malnutrition, dehydration, and despair. The captain of the ship, George Long, and his crew, far from being sympathetic to the plight of their passengers, subjected them to cruel treatment and extortion, demanding additional payment for the meagre provisions they provided.

It was in this grim atmosphere that the Princess Augusta finally approached the coast of North America, the desperate passengers straining their eyes to catch a glimpse of the land they had dreamed of for so long. However, their joy was short-lived, for the treacherous waters surrounding Block Island would claim the ship as their own. On December 27, 1738, the Princess Augusta ran aground on a sandbar off the northern coast of the island, its hull torn open by the jagged rocks that lay hidden beneath the waves.

The wreck of the Princess Augusta quickly attracted the attention of the island's inhabitants, who set out in boats to reach the doomed vessel. As they approached the ship, they were confronted by the horrifying sight of the emaciated and terrified passengers, many of whom were barely clinging to life. The islanders, moved by compassion and a sense of duty, began a heroic rescue operation, bringing the survivors to the safety of their homes and tending to their injuries and illnesses.

But the story does not end there, for amid the chaos and confusion of the rescue, a sinister act would forever change the course of the Princess Augusta's legacy. It is said that a group of islanders, driven by greed and avarice, seized upon the opportunity presented by the wreck to loot the ship of its valuable cargo. As the terrified passengers looked on, the looters set fire to the vessel, perhaps in an attempt to cover their tracks or to hasten the process of scavenging the wreckage. Whatever their motives, the flames quickly engulfed the Princess Augusta, transforming the once-majestic ship into a blazing inferno that illuminated the night sky.

The heart-wrenching screams of those trapped onboard, unable to escape the inferno, echoed across the water, haunting the islanders who had tried to save them. It is said that the fire burned so hot and so brightly that it could be seen for miles around, casting an eerie glow upon the waters of Block Island Sound. As the flames consumed the ship, the Princess Augusta's tragic end was seared into the memories of those who bore witness to the horrifying spectacle. When the fire finally subsided, all that remained of the ship was a charred and smouldering wreck, a grim testament to the terrible events that had unfolded.

In the years that followed, the tale of the Princess Augusta became the stuff of legend on Block Island and beyond, the story of the ghost ship and its fiery demise passed down through generations. And as the years turned into decades, and the decades into centuries, the legend of the Princess Augusta took on a supernatural dimension, with reports of a chilling phenomenon known as the Palatine Light.

The Palatine Light is said to appear on dark and stormy nights, a ghostly apparition of the blazing ship that flickers and dances upon the waves, its haunting glow visible for miles around. Many believe that this eerie phenomenon is the restless spirit of the Princess Augusta, forever doomed to relive its fiery destruction as a spectral reminder of the greed, cruelty, and tragedy that marked its final moments.

Eyewitness accounts of the Palatine Light abound, with sailors, fishermen, and islanders alike claiming to have seen the ghostly ship burning on the horizon. Some say that the apparition is accompanied by the mournful wails of the passengers who perished in the flames, their cries carried upon the wind like the anguished whispers of the damned.

Others believe that the Palatine Light is not merely the restless spirit of the Princess Augusta, but also a harbinger of doom, a portent of disaster for those who encounter it. Numerous shipwrecks have been reported in the waters surrounding Block Island, and many believe that the ghostly fire is a manifestation of the malevolent forces that lie in wait beneath the waves, ready to claim the unwary.

But what is the truth behind the legend of the Princess Augusta and the Palatine Light? Are the tales of the haunted ship and its ghostly apparition merely the product of superstition and imagination, or is there a darker and more sinister reality at work? Some historians and paranormal investigators have sought to unravel the mystery, delving into the archives and examining the accounts of those who have claimed to witness the eerie phenomenon.

While the exact details of the Princess Augusta's tragic fate remain shrouded in mystery, it is clear that the legend has left an indelible mark on the collective consciousness of those who live and work on the waters of the Atlantic Ocean. The story of the ghost ship and its fiery demise continues to captivate and terrify in equal measure, a chilling reminder of the darker side of human nature and the unfathomable forces that govern the sea.

Whether fact or fiction, the haunting tale of the Princess Augusta and the Palatine Light serves as a cautionary tale for all who venture out upon the vast and treacherous waters of the Atlantic. It is a story that speaks to the deepest fears and darkest instincts that reside within the human heart, a testament to the enduring power of legends and the timeless allure of the supernatural.

As you continue your voyage through the haunted waters of history, remember the tale of the Princess Augusta and its fiery end. Let it serve as a reminder of the dangers that lurk beneath the surface of our understanding, and the ghostly whispers that echo through the ages, beckoning us to explore the unknown. For in the dark and stormy waters of the past, there lie secrets that defy comprehension, and mysteries that are destined to remain forever unsolved.

The Ourang Medan: A Cryptic SOS and Ghostly Crew

The ocean, with its vast and seemingly endless expanse, has long been a source of both wonder and terror for those who venture upon its waters. Among the countless tales of ghostly vessels and maritime hauntings, few stories are as chilling and enigmatic as that of the Ourang Medan, a ship found adrift with its deceased crew and the paranormal theories that surround it. As we delve into the murky depths of this haunting mystery, we must confront the eerie spectres of the past and the darkest corners of the human psyche.

The story of the Ourang Medan begins in the late 1940s, when a series of cryptic SOS messages were intercepted by numerous ships sailing in the Strait of Malacca, an important and busy shipping route between the Indonesian archipelago and the Malay Peninsula. The messages, sent in Morse code, were a desperate plea for help from the Dutch freighter Ourang Medan, claiming that the ship's crew, including the captain, were dead and that the vessel was adrift. The messages ended with a chilling and enigmatic statement: "I die."

Alarmed by the urgency and cryptic nature of the distress calls, nearby ships raced to the aid of the Ourang Medan, searching for any sign of the stricken vessel. It was the American merchant ship, the Silver Star, that first located the Ourang Medan, drifting aimlessly upon the calm waters of the strait. As the crew of the Silver Star approached the ghostly vessel, they were immediately struck by a palpable sense of dread and unease, as if the very air around the ship was charged with a malignant energy.

Upon boarding the Ourang Medan, the crew of the Silver Star were confronted by a horrifying scene that would haunt them for the rest of their lives. The Dutch freighter's crew lay dead, their bodies sprawled across the deck in twisted and unnatural poses, their faces frozen in expressions of abject terror. Even the ship's dog, a faithful and loyal companion to the crew, lay dead, its snarling visage a testament to the unseen horrors that had befallen the ill-fated vessel.

As the crew of the Silver Star searched the Ourang Medan for any survivors or clues as to what had caused the ship's demise, they were struck by an oppressive and unnatural heat that seemed to radiate from the very core of the ship. This stifling atmosphere, combined with the eerie silence that hung over the vessel, only served to heighten the sense of dread and foreboding that gripped the rescue party.

It was during this search that the crew of the Silver Star made a chilling discovery. The ship's cargo hold, which should have contained a valuable cargo of rubber and tin, was instead filled with an assortment of mysterious and unmarked crates, the contents of which would never be revealed. Was the Ourang Medan's true purpose a clandestine and nefarious mission, one that would ultimately lead to its doom?

With no survivors and no clear explanation for the horrifying scene that had unfolded aboard the Ourang Medan, the crew of the Silver Star made the fateful decision to tow the ghostly vessel back to port. But as they prepared to embark on this arduous journey, a sudden and violent explosion rocked the Ourang Medan, sending a plume of smoke and fire high into the sky. The ship, now engulfed in flames, quickly sank beneath the waves, taking its secrets and the remains of its crew with it to the bottom of the ocean.

In the years that followed, the story of the Ourang Medan would capture the imagination of the world, becoming a source of endless speculation and intrigue for both paranormal enthusiasts and maritime historians alike. Theories abound as to the cause of the mysterious deaths aboard the ship, with some suggesting that the crew had succumbed to a deadly and undetected gas leak, while others point to the possibility of foul play or even a mutiny gone awry. But among the various explanations, there are those who believe that the events aboard the Ourang Medan were the result of something far more sinister and otherworldly.

One such theory is that the ship and its crew had become the unwitting victims of a malevolent and supernatural force, perhaps even a curse or demonic possession that had driven the crew to madness and death. Proponents of this theory point to the eerie nature of the SOS messages, the unnatural heat that pervaded the vessel, and the horrifying expressions of terror etched upon the faces of the deceased crew as evidence of the ship's ghostly and supernatural nature.

Others believe that the mysterious cargo held within the Ourang Medan's hold may have been the source of the ship's haunting and tragic fate. Could the unmarked crates have contained some form of cursed or haunted artefact, an object imbued with the power to bring about the crew's untimely demise? Or perhaps the cargo was something far more dangerous and forbidden, a secret so dark and malevolent that it had attracted the attention of forces beyond our understanding.

Another theory that has gained traction among UFO enthusiasts is that the Ourang Medan may have encountered an extraterrestrial presence during its fateful voyage, with some even suggesting that the ship's crew had been subjected to a horrifying and lethal experiment at the hands of an alien intelligence. This theory, while undoubtedly far-fetched, is supported by the mysterious nature of the ship's cargo, the bizarre and inexplicable circumstances surrounding the crew's deaths, and the sudden and violent explosion that sent the vessel to its watery grave.

Despite the numerous theories and conjectures that have been put forth, the true cause of the Ourang Medan's tragic end remains a mystery, a chilling enigma that continues to haunt the annals of maritime history. The story of the ghostly ship and its doomed crew serves as a stark reminder of the unfathomable depths of the ocean and the unknown dangers that lurk within its vast and mysterious expanse.

As we continue our journey through the haunted waters of history's most enigmatic vessels, let the chilling tale of the Ourang Medan be a cautionary tale, a grim reminder of the terrors that await those who dare to venture too far into the unknown. For within the vast and uncharted depths of the sea, there are forces and phenomena that defy explanation, and secrets that are best left undisturbed.

In the world of haunted ships and boats, the Ourang Medan stands as a particularly chilling and intriguing mystery, one that invites speculation and wonder in equal measure. It is a story that resonates with our deepest fears and darkest curiosities, a tale that reminds us that the ocean, for all its beauty and majesty, is a realm of mystery, danger, and the unexplained. And as we navigate the haunted waters of our own lives, it is a tale that will continue to haunt and inspire us, a ghostly beacon shining through the fog of uncertainty and the depths of our collective imagination.

The HMS Eurydice: The Haunted Warship of the Solent

The waters of the Solent, a strait separating the Isle of Wight from the southern coast of England, have long been the setting for countless maritime tales. Among these, one stands out as particularly haunting and tragic: the story of the HMS Eurydice. This Victorian-era warship met its grim fate in 1878, taking with it the lives of over 300 crew members. The Eurydice's ghostly legacy continues to cast a dark shadow over the waters of the Solent, with numerous accounts of paranormal encounters that have both intrigued and terrified those who have crossed its path.

The HMS Eurydice, a 26-gun Royal Navy corvette, was commissioned in 1843 and served as a training vessel for naval cadets. This magnificent ship was named after the mythical Greek character Eurydice, the wife of Orpheus, who tragically died and was lost to the underworld. Little did anyone know that the ship's namesake would foreshadow its own tragic destiny.

Under the command of Captain Marcus Augustus Stanley Hare, the Eurydice set sail on her final voyage in November 1877, embarking on a journey to Bermuda and back. The months-long voyage was meant to provide valuable training and experience for the young cadets on board. As they traversed the Atlantic Ocean, the crew faced both fair weather and raging storms, successfully navigating the treacherous waters with the skills they had honed during their training.

On the fateful day of March 24, 1878, the Eurydice was en route back to her homeport in Portsmouth. The sky was clear, and the ship glided effortlessly across the calm waters of the Solent. As the sun began to set, however, a sudden and fierce snowstorm descended upon the ship, catching the crew off guard. The intensity of the storm made it nearly impossible for them to see, let alone control the ship's movements.

Within minutes, the Eurydice was engulfed in the storm's icy grip, and the once-calm waters had transformed into a tumultuous sea. In the chaos that ensued, the ship's sails were caught in a powerful gust, and the vessel was violently thrown onto its side. Water rushed into the ship's open hatches, causing it to sink rapidly. Despite the crew's valiant efforts to right the ship, it was ultimately a futile endeavor. The Eurydice, along with the majority of her crew, was swallowed by the merciless waves.

The sinking of the Eurydice sent shockwaves through the British naval community. The disaster was one of the worst in the history of the Royal Navy, with 318 lives lost. In the wake of the tragedy, the ship's wreckage was salvaged, and a court-martial absolved Captain Hare of any wrongdoing. The true cause of the sinking remained shrouded in mystery and speculation, fueling rumors of supernatural forces at work.

It wasn't long after the disaster that people began reporting strange occurrences in the waters of the Solent. Locals and sailors alike claimed to have seen a ghostly ship, eerily similar in appearance to the Eurydice, gliding silently across the water. Witnesses described the vessel as being surrounded by an unnatural fog, and some even claimed to have heard the cries of the doomed crew echoing through the mist.

One of the most famous accounts of the Eurydice's ghostly presence comes from the 20th century, when Prince Edward, later known as King Edward VIII, was serving aboard the HMS Cadmus. The prince and his fellow officers claimed to have spotted the spectral ship off the coast of the Isle of Wight, bearing an eerie resemblance to the ill-fated Eurydice. As they watched in disbelief, the phantom vessel appeared to be struggling against a raging storm, with its crew desperately trying to control the sails. Moments later, the ship vanished into the mist, leaving no trace of its presence. This chilling encounter, experienced by such a high-profile figure, only served to solidify the legend of the haunted warship.

Over the years, numerous other sightings and encounters with the ghostly Eurydice have been reported, each one adding to the ship's tragic legacy. Some claim to have seen the spectre of Captain Hare, standing stoically on the ship's deck, while others have reported hearing the heart-wrenching wails of the lost crew members carried by the wind.

Despite extensive efforts to debunk the myth or find a rational explanation for these sightings, no conclusive evidence has ever been presented to disprove the existence of the haunted Eurydice. As such, the ghostly warship has become an enduring part of local folklore, captivating the imagination of those who hear its tale.

Today, the story of the HMS Eurydice serves as a chilling reminder of the unpredictable and unforgiving nature of the sea, as well as the bravery and sacrifice of those who served aboard her. The haunted warship of the Solent continues to captivate and terrify sailors and locals alike, with each new encounter adding to the legend that has persisted for over a century.

The Carroll A. Deering: The Bermuda Triangle's Ghost Ship

The Bermuda Triangle, a roughly triangular region of the Atlantic Ocean situated between Miami, Bermuda, and Puerto Rico, has long been shrouded in mystery and superstition. Countless ships and aircraft have disappeared without a trace within its boundaries, sparking both scientific inquiry and paranormal speculation. One of the most enigmatic and haunting stories to emerge from this treacherous region involves a five-masted commercial schooner named the Carroll A. Deering.

Launched in 1919, the Carroll A. Deering was a stunning example of early 20th-century shipbuilding, boasting a sleek wooden hull, towering masts, and expansive sails. She was named after the son of her owner, G.G. Deering, a wealthy

American businessman. With a crew of eleven, the Deering set sail under the command of Captain William H. Merritt on August 22, 1920, from Norfolk, Virginia, bound for Rio de Janeiro, Brazil, with a cargo of coal.

The voyage to Brazil proceeded smoothly, and the Deering arrived in Rio de Janeiro on September 9, 1920. However, during the ship's stay in port, Captain Merritt fell gravely ill and was unable to continue as the ship's master. Reluctantly, Merritt and his son, Sewall, who served as first mate, disembarked, and Captain Willis B. Wormell, a seasoned mariner with years of experience under his belt, took command of the vessel. Charles B. McLellan was appointed as the new first mate, and the Deering resumed her voyage, departing Rio de Janeiro on December 2, 1920, for the return trip to Norfolk.

On January 29, 1921, the Deering passed by Barbados, where Captain Wormell met with an old friend, Captain Hugh Norton of the SS Hewitt. The two men shared a meal and discussed their respective journeys. Wormell expressed concerns about his crew's behaviour and loyalty, particularly that of first mate McLellan. Norton advised Wormell to take precautions and maintain vigilance, and the two captains parted ways, each returning to his respective ship.

Little did Captain Norton know that his conversation with Wormell would be the last known contact anyone would have with the crew of the Carroll A. Deering. What transpired between that fateful meeting and the ship's eventual discovery is a chilling mystery that remains unsolved to this day.

On January 31, 1921, the Deering was spotted by the Cape Lookout Lightship in North Carolina. The ship's behaviour was erratic, and the crew appeared disorganised. The lightship's keeper, Captain Jacobson, attempted to communicate with the schooner, but the man who responded seemed unfamiliar with maritime signalling. As the Deering continued on its peculiar course, Captain Jacobson noted that the ship's navigational equipment appeared to be missing, further deepening the sense of unease surrounding the vessel.

Two days later, on February 2, 1921, the Carroll A. Deering was found aground on Diamond Shoals, off Cape Hatteras, North Carolina. The ship's sails were set, but there was no sign of the crew or their personal belongings. The ship's log, navigational instruments, lifeboats, and galley supplies were all missing, and the ship's steering gear had been deliberately disabled. A thorough investigation ensued, led by the United States Coast Guard and various other government agencies. However, despite their best efforts, no trace of the crew or any concrete explanation for the ship's abandonment was ever found.

The enigmatic fate of the Carroll A. Deering has since become the subject of numerous paranormal theories and speculations. Some attribute the crew's disappearance to the supernatural forces believed to be at play within the Bermuda Triangle, while others suggest that piracy, mutiny, or even a rogue wave may have played a role in the ship's tragic end. Over the years, the story of the Deering has been woven into the tapestry of nautical folklore, earning the vessel the moniker of "The Bermuda Triangle's Ghost Ship."

One popular theory suggests that the crew of the Deering fell victim to the Sargasso Sea's legendary ghost pirates. According to maritime lore, the Sargasso Sea, which lies within the Bermuda Triangle, is home to a band of spectral pirates who prey on unwary sailors, leading their vessels astray and condemning the crew to a watery grave. Proponents of this theory argue that the Deering's dishevelled appearance, coupled with the missing navigational equipment, is evidence of a ghostly pirate encounter.

Another theory points to the possibility of mutiny aboard the

Deering. Given Captain Wormell's concerns about his crew's loyalty, particularly that of first mate McLellan, some speculate that the crew staged a mutiny, resulting in the ship's abandonment. The removal of the ship's log, navigational instruments, and lifeboats suggests that the crew may have deliberately scuttled the ship and escaped in the lifeboats, leaving the vessel to drift into the treacherous waters of Diamond Shoals.

A third hypothesis, rooted in scientific reasoning, posits that the Deering and her crew were the unfortunate victims of a massive rogue wave. Rogue waves are extraordinarily large and unpredictable waves that can appear suddenly in otherwise calm seas, posing a significant threat to ships and their crews. It's plausible that a rogue wave struck the Deering with such force that it dislodged the crew's personal belongings, damaged the ship's steering gear, and swept the crew overboard, leaving the vessel to drift aimlessly until it ran aground on Diamond Shoals.

Despite the myriad theories surrounding the fate of the Carroll A. Deering, no definitive explanation for the ship's abandonment and the crew's disappearance has ever been determined. The ship's remains were eventually dynamited to prevent it from becoming a navigational hazard, but the vessel's ghostly legacy endures. Over the years, numerous sailors have reported sightings of a mysterious five-masted schooner in the vicinity of Diamond Shoals, with some even claiming to have witnessed ghostly figures on its deck, forever plying the haunted waters of the Bermuda Triangle.

The haunting tale of the Carroll A. Deering serves as a chilling reminder of the perils and uncertainties that have plagued seafarers for centuries. It's a story that continues to captivate and mystify, inviting us to ponder the depths of human courage, the unfathomable power of nature, and the tantalising allure of the unknown. As the Deering's enigmatic fate remains shrouded in mystery, the ship stands as a testament to the enduring human fascination with the paranormal, an eerie beacon that draws us ever deeper into the realm of nautical nightmares and paranormal encounters at sea.

The SS Watertown: Faces in the Waves

The sea holds many secrets, and the SS Watertown is no exception. This seemingly ordinary oil tanker was witness to a tragic event in 1924 that gave birth to one of the most chilling and enigmatic maritime ghost stories of the 20th century. As we delve into the haunting tale of the SS Watertown, we will encounter the eerie apparitions of two crew members whose ghostly faces were spotted in the waves following their untimely deaths, leaving those who witnessed the phenomenon forever changed.

To better understand the context of the haunting, it is important to first acquaint ourselves with the vessel in question. The SS Watertown was an American oil tanker built in 1919 by the Bethlehem Shipbuilding Corporation in Quincy, Massachusetts. Operated by the Standard Oil Company, the tanker was tasked with transporting oil between ports along the East and West

Coasts of the United States, as well as voyages to the Far East. In December 1924, the Watertown was en route from New Orleans to the Panama Canal, continuing onward to San Francisco.

Tragedy struck on December 4, 1924, when two crew members, James Courtney and Michael Meehan, were overcome by fumes while cleaning an empty cargo tank. Their fellow crew members, who were initially unaware of the situation, soon discovered the men lying unconscious on the tank floor. Despite their best efforts to revive Courtney and Meehan, the toxic fumes had already claimed their lives. In accordance with maritime tradition, the deceased crew members were buried at sea, their bodies committed to the depths of the ocean on December 5.

It was only a few days after the burial at sea that the crew of the SS Watertown began to report strange sightings. On December 7, as the tanker made its way through the Gulf of Mexico, several crew members claimed to see the faces of James Courtney and Michael Meehan in the waves that trailed behind the vessel. These ghostly visages appeared to be in a state of distress, their expressions contorted with pain and anguish. The apparitions were not fleeting; they remained visible for several minutes before slowly fading from view, leaving the crew in a state of shock and disbelief.

Word of the sightings spread quickly among the crew, and soon, even those who had not personally witnessed the apparitions began to experience a palpable sense of dread on board the Watertown. As the tanker continued on its journey, the faces of Courtney and Meehan appeared repeatedly in the waves, their haunting presence a grim reminder of the tragic accident that had befallen them. By the time the Watertown reached the Panama Canal, the entire crew was on edge, anxiously scanning the waters for any sign of the ghostly faces.

Upon arriving in the Canal Zone, the ship's captain, Keith Tracy, decided to report the sightings to his superiors at the Standard Oil Company. He was concerned not only for the emotional well-being of his crew but also for the potential damage the haunting could cause to the company's reputation. The executives at Standard Oil, sceptical of the paranormal claims, instructed Captain Tracy to document the apparitions with photographic evidence.

In January 1925, the Watertown left the Panama Canal and continued its voyage to San Francisco. Armed with a camera, Captain Tracy and his chief officer, James S. Whitmore, waited for the ghostly faces to reappear. When the apparitions finally emerged in the waves, Tracy and Whitmore quickly snapped several photographs, hoping to capture evidence of the supernatural phenomena. Once the Watertown reached San Francisco, the photographs were developed and sent to the Standard Oil headquarters in New York.

The resulting images were nothing short of astonishing. The photographs clearly showed the faces of James Courtney and Michael Meehan in the waves, their anguished expressions and ghostly visages captured for all to see. In an attempt to ensure the validity of the images, the Standard Oil Company enlisted the help of an independent investigator to examine the photographs. After a thorough analysis, the investigator concluded that the images had not been tampered with, lending credence to the claims of the Watertown's crew.

As news of the haunting photographs spread, the story of the SS Watertown quickly gained international attention. The tale of the ghostly faces in the waves resonated with people from all walks of life, becoming a symbol of the tragic consequences of industrial accidents and the enduring bond between shipmates. The photographs themselves became an iconic representation of maritime hauntings, earning a place in the annals of paranormal history.

Despite the attention that the haunting of the SS Watertown garnered, the vessel continued to operate as an oil tanker for many years after the tragic events of 1924. In fact, the ship served throughout World War II, playing a vital role in the transportation of much-needed oil supplies to Allied forces. The Watertown was eventually decommissioned in 1947 and scrapped in 1950, bringing an end to the ship's storied history.

The tale of the SS Watertown and its ghostly apparitions remains a chilling reminder of the dangers that maritime workers faced in the early 20th century. The haunting story also serves as a testament to the enduring power of human connection, as the spirits of James Courtney and Michael Meehan seemingly refused to leave their shipmates behind, even in death.

Over the years, the haunting of the SS Watertown has been the subject of much speculation and debate. Some paranormal enthusiasts believe that the ghostly faces in the waves were a manifestation of the immense grief and guilt felt by the crew, who were unable to save their fellow shipmates from the deadly fumes. Others argue that the apparitions were a result of the restless spirits of Courtney and Meehan, unable to move on due to the tragic nature of their deaths.

Regardless of the true nature of the haunting, the story of the SS Watertown serves as a chilling reminder of the mysteries that lurk beneath the surface of the sea. As we explore the depths of human fascination with the paranormal, we are left to wonder what other ghostly secrets remain hidden within the hulls of ships like the Watertown, waiting to be discovered by those brave enough to venture into the haunted waters of history's most enigmatic vessels.

The Admiral Nelson: The Haunted Tall Ship

The vast oceans and their seemingly infinite depths have long been the inspiration for tales of the supernatural, with stories of ghostly ships and their spectral crews forever haunting the imaginations of sailors and landlubbers alike. Of these nautical legends, few are as enigmatic and chilling as the tale of the Admiral Nelson, a Swedish tall ship whose haunted history continues to captivate and terrify those who dare to delve into its murky past.

Built in the late 18th century, the Admiral Nelson was a stunning example of the wooden sailing vessels that once dominated the seas. With her lofty masts and billowing sails, she was an impressive sight to behold, inspiring both awe and envy in the hearts of her contemporaries. Originally commissioned as a merchant vessel, the ship's sturdy construction and spacious cargo holds made her an ideal choice for long voyages across the

Atlantic, ferrying goods between the Old World and the New.

However, it wasn't long before the Admiral Nelson's storied past took a dark and sinister turn. During the height of the Napoleonic Wars, the ship was commandeered by the Swedish navy, which sought to bolster its fleet in the face of mounting pressure from the British Royal Navy. It was during this tumultuous period that the first whispers of ghostly activity began to echo through the ship's timbers.

The ship's conversion into a naval vessel brought with it a host of modifications, including the addition of several cannons and a complement of marines tasked with manning them. As the Admiral Nelson was plunged into the chaos of naval warfare, her crew began to report eerie occurrences and inexplicable phenomena that would come to define her as one of the most haunted ships in maritime history.

One such tale comes from a young sailor named Anders, who was stationed aboard the Admiral Nelson during a particularly harrowing engagement with a British frigate. As cannon fire tore through the air and splintered the ship's wooden hull, Anders found himself pinned beneath a fallen beam, his cries for help drowned out by the cacophony of battle. As he lay there, trapped and terrified, he claimed to have seen the spectral figure of a woman in a flowing white gown, her eyes locked onto his as she drifted through the smoke and chaos of the fighting.

Though his account was initially met with scepticism, Anders' tale soon gained traction among the crew as more and more sailors reported similar encounters with the mysterious apparition. The woman, who came to be known as the Lady in White, was said to appear only during the most desperate moments of battle, as if drawn to the suffering and turmoil of the men she haunted.

As the war raged on and the Admiral Nelson continued to carve a bloody path through the waters of the Atlantic, the Lady in White became an ever-present specter, her ghostly visage haunting the dreams and waking hours of the beleaguered crew. Some began to speculate that she was the spirit of a long-lost lover, her soul forever bound to the ship by a tragic and unbreakable bond. Others believed her to be a vengeful wraith, her wrath ignited by the carnage and destruction wrought by the vessel she was cursed to haunt.

In the years that followed the Napoleonic Wars, the Admiral Nelson was returned to her original purpose as a merchant ship, her cannons and marines replaced by bales of cotton and barrels of rum. But the dark legacy of her time in the navy was not so easily cast off, and the tales of the Lady in White persisted, her ghostly presence a chilling reminder of the ship's bloody past.

Over the years, as the ship changed hands and plied new trade routes, the sightings of the Lady in White continued unabated, with each new crew adding their own accounts of encounters with the enigmatic spirit. From the tropical waters of the Caribbean to the icy reaches of the Arctic, the ghostly figure seemed to follow the Admiral Nelson wherever she sailed, her haunting gaze a constant presence in the lives of those who served aboard her.

As the 19th century gave way to the 20th, the age of wooden sailing ships drew to a close, their once-imposing forms overshadowed by the ironclads and steamships that came to dominate the world's oceans. The Admiral Nelson, however, refused to fade quietly into the annals of history. Instead, the ship was purchased by a wealthy Swedish businessman, who sought to restore her to her former glory and preserve her as a living testament to a bygone era.

Over the course of several years, the Admiral Nelson underwent a painstaking restoration process, her timbers carefully repaired and her sails lovingly stitched back together. It was during this period of renewal that the ship's haunted reputation began to pique the interest of paranormal investigators, who flocked to her in the hopes of catching a glimpse of the legendary Lady in White.

Among these investigators was the renowned psychic medium, Ingrid Larsson, who claimed to have made contact with the spirit during a nighttime vigil aboard the ship. According to Larsson, the Lady in White was a woman named Elsa, who had lost her life aboard the ship in the late 18th century. Elsa had been a passenger on the ship, travelling to meet her fiancé in the New World, but tragedy struck when she was accidentally killed during a violent storm. Distraught and unable to move on, her spirit remained tethered to the ship, her eternal wandering fueled by the sorrow and longing that had plagued her in life.

With this revelation, the legend of the Admiral Nelson and her ghostly passenger took on a new dimension, the chilling tales of the Lady in White now imbued with a sense of profound tragedy. As word of Larsson's findings spread, the ship became a magnet for ghost hunters and paranormal enthusiasts, eager to experience the haunted vessel for themselves.

In the years that followed, the Admiral Nelson embarked on a new chapter in her storied history, serving as a floating museum and event space. Visitors from around the world flocked to her, drawn not only by her impressive appearance but also by the eerie allure of her haunted past. Within her wooden hull, the spectral figure of the Lady in White continued to roam, her presence a constant reminder of the ship's dark and turbulent history.

But the Admiral Nelson's haunted legacy is about more than just ghostly sightings and chilling legends. It is also a testament to the power of the human imagination and our enduring fascination with the unknown. From the earliest days of seafaring, sailors have shared stories of supernatural encounters and otherworldly phenomena, their tales of haunted ships and ghostly crews serving as a means of making sense of the vast, unknowable depths that surrounded them.

In this way, the story of the Admiral Nelson and the Lady in White is a reflection of our collective desire to explore the mysteries of the world around us and to seek out the hidden truths that lie just beyond the horizon. It is a reminder that even in an age of advanced technology and scientific discovery, there is still room for wonder and speculation, for the eerie tales and spine-tingling legends that have long captivated the human spirit.

The SS Great Eastern: Iron Leviathan's Phantom Passengers

The annals of maritime history are filled with tales of haunted ships and ghostly apparitions, their stories woven together by the threads of human tragedy, mystery, and the inexorable passage of time. One such tale is that of the SS Great Eastern, a colossal engineering marvel that was once the largest ship ever built, and whose haunted history has captivated the imagination of generations.

Designed by the visionary engineer Isambard Kingdom Brunel, the SS Great Eastern was an iron-hulled behemoth, a symbol of the Industrial Revolution and a testament to humanity's relentless pursuit of progress. Launched in 1858, the ship was a technological marvel of her time, boasting an innovative combination of steam engines and paddle wheels that allowed her to traverse the world's oceans with unparalleled speed and power.

However, the SS Great Eastern's remarkable engineering achievements were matched by a dark and troubled history, marred by misfortune, catastrophe, and a series of inexplicable ghostly encounters that would come to define her as one of the most haunted vessels ever to sail the high seas.

From the very beginning, the SS Great Eastern seemed to be beset by ill omens and cursed by misfortune. During her tumultuous construction, several workers were killed in a series of tragic accidents, their untimely deaths casting a pall of dread over the shipyard. As the ship's launch approached, whispers of ghostly sightings began to circulate among the crew, with many claiming to have seen the spectral figures of the deceased workers roaming the decks, their restless spirits forever bound to the iron leviathan they had helped to create.

Once the ship was completed and ready for her maiden voyage, it was hoped that the dark cloud that had hung over her would finally dissipate. However, the SS Great Eastern's first journey was marred by yet another tragedy, as one of the ship's stokers was killed in a horrific explosion. This tragic event would prove to be just the first of many accidents and misfortunes that would plague the vessel throughout her ill-fated career.

As the SS Great Eastern traversed the globe, her crew bore witness to a litany of ghostly encounters and inexplicable phenomena, their chilling accounts fueling the ship's haunted reputation. Among the most persistent of these spectral sightings were the phantom passengers who seemed to haunt the ship's luxurious saloons and staterooms.

These ghostly figures, dressed in the finery of a bygone age, were said to glide silently through the ship's opulent corridors, their hollow gazes betraying the anguish and sorrow that seemed to bind them to the vessel. As the crew shared their stories of these eerie apparitions, rumours began to circulate that they were the spirits of passengers who had perished aboard the ship, their souls unable to find peace in the afterlife.

The tales of the SS Great Eastern's phantom passengers were not confined to her crew, however. Over the years, as the ship carried countless travellers across the world's oceans, many of her passengers would also report encounters with the ghostly figures, their chilling experiences adding to the ever-growing body of evidence that seemed to confirm the vessel's haunted status.

In one particularly harrowing account, a young woman named Emily described how, as she lay in her stateroom one stormy night, she was awakened by the sound of a door creaking open. As she looked up, she was confronted by the spectral figure of a woman in a flowing white gown, her eyes locked onto Emily's as she drifted silently into the room. Terrified, Emily watched as the ghostly apparition passed through the opposite wall, disappearing into the darkness beyond.

As the SS Great Eastern continued to ply her trade across the world's oceans, her haunted reputation grew, drawing the attention of both paranormal enthusiasts and sceptical investigators alike. One such investigator was a renowned psychic medium named Charles Wentworth, who sought to uncover the truth behind the ship's ghostly passengers and bring an end to the haunting that seemed to have gripped the vessel.

Wentworth spent several weeks aboard the SS Great Eastern, conducting a series of seances and attempting to communicate with the spirits that were believed to haunt the ship. Through these sessions, he claimed to have made contact with several of the phantom passengers, who revealed to him that they were the souls of individuals who had met tragic ends aboard the ship, their spirits unable to move on due to the unresolved nature of their deaths.

Armed with this knowledge, Wentworth sought to help the spirits find peace, conducting a series of elaborate rituals designed to release them from their earthly bonds and allow them to pass into the afterlife. Although it is impossible to say for certain whether his efforts were successful, there are those who claim that the ghostly sightings aboard the SS Great Eastern diminished following Wentworth's interventions, suggesting that the spirits of the phantom passengers may have finally found the peace they so desperately sought.

Despite the efforts of Wentworth and others like him, the SS Great Eastern's haunted reputation would continue to grow over the course of her long and troubled career. As the ship aged and her once-gleaming hull began to rust and decay, her ghostly passengers seemed to become an ever more integral part of her identity, their spectral forms a haunting reminder of the tragedies and misfortunes that had marred her history.

Ultimately, the SS Great Eastern would meet an ignominious end, her once-impressive form reduced to scrap metal and her mighty engines silenced forever. However, her ghostly legacy would endure, the tales of her phantom passengers and haunted history continuing to captivate the imaginations of those who seek to explore the mysterious world of maritime hauntings.

The story of the SS Great Eastern and her ghostly passengers serves as a powerful reminder of humanity's enduring fascination with the paranormal and our insatiable desire to uncover the secrets that lie hidden within the shadowy recesses of our past. As we delve into the chilling tales of haunted ships and ghostly encounters that populate the pages of this book, we are reminded that the world is a place of mystery and wonder, where the ghosts of our history continue to cast their spectral shadows over the present.

The MV Joyita: The Pacific's Vanishing Ghost Ship

The vast expanse of the Pacific Ocean, with its seemingly endless horizon and unfathomable depths, has long been a source of fascination and fear for those who dare to venture across its treacherous waters. This mighty ocean has given birth to countless tales of ghost ships and vanishing vessels, their chilling stories serving as a stark reminder of the power and mystery of the sea. One such tale is that of the MV Joyita, a vessel whose enigmatic disappearance and subsequent discovery would come to be known as one of the most baffling maritime mysteries of the 20th century.

The MV Joyita was a modest wooden-hulled motor vessel, built in 1931 as a luxury yacht for a wealthy Los Angeles businessman. Over the years, she passed through numerous owners and served various purposes, including a stint as a US Navy patrol boat during World War II. By the early 1950s, the

Joyita had found her way to the South Pacific, where she was employed as a trading and fishing vessel, plying the remote waters between Fiji and Samoa.

On October 3, 1955, the MV Joyita set sail from the port of Apia in Samoa, bound for the Fijian capital of Suva. On board were 25 souls, a motley crew of traders, fishers, and passengers, each seeking to make their fortune in the far-flung islands of the Pacific. The voyage was expected to take no more than 48 hours, but as the days passed and the Joyita failed to arrive at her destination, concern began to grow for the fate of the vessel and her crew.

An extensive search and rescue operation was launched, with ships and aircraft scouring thousands of square miles of ocean in an effort to locate the missing vessel. Despite these efforts, the MV Joyita seemed to have vanished without a trace, her disappearance only serving to deepen the mystery and fuel speculation as to her fate.

It would be more than a month before the MV Joyita would finally be found, her battered and waterlogged hull discovered adrift some 600 miles off her intended course. The vessel was listing heavily to one side, her decks awash with water, and her interior in a state of disarray. Most chillingly, however, was the discovery that the Joyita was completely abandoned, her crew and passengers nowhere to be found.

The circumstances of the Joyita's discovery were as baffling as they were eerie. The vessel's lifeboats were missing, suggesting that the crew had abandoned ship at some point during the voyage. However, there was no sign of the passengers, their belongings, or any of the cargo the ship had been carrying. Furthermore, an examination of the vessel's engines revealed that they were inoperable, yet the Joyita's radio was still functioning, its distress signal never having been activated.

The mystery of the MV Joyita's disappearance and the fate of her crew and passengers has never been fully explained, with countless theories and explanations put forth in an effort to make sense of the enigma. Among the most persistent of these theories is the notion that the vessel was beset by some form of paranormal activity, her unexplained disappearance and subsequent discovery serving as evidence of a supernatural force at work.

Over the years, numerous accounts have emerged of ghostly encounters and strange phenomena aboard the MV Joyita, both before and after her mysterious vanishing. Prior to her fateful voyage, several crew members had reported experiencing an inexplicable sense of dread while aboard the vessel, with some even claiming to have seen spectral figures lurking in the shadows of the ship's cramped quarters.

Following the Joyita's discovery and eventual return to service, her haunted reputation only grew, with many sailors refusing to set foot on her decks, fearing the wrath of the spirits that were said to linger within her hull. Despite numerous attempts to restore the vessel and put her back to work, the MV Joyita's haunted legacy proved to be an insurmountable obstacle, her name forever linked with the eerie tales of ghost ships and paranormal encounters that abound in maritime lore.

Those who did dare to sail aboard the Joyita in the years following her mysterious disappearance reported a variety of strange occurrences, ranging from inexplicable cold spots and unexplained noises to chilling apparitions and disembodied voices. Some even claimed to have seen the spectral forms of the vessel's missing crew and passengers, their ghostly figures forever trapped within the confines of the ill-fated ship.

One particularly chilling account comes from a fisherman named

Taniela, who spent several months aboard the Joyita as part of a fishing expedition in the late 1950s. Taniela claimed that, on more than one occasion, he had witnessed the ghostly figure of a woman standing on the ship's deck, staring out into the distance as if searching for something or someone lost at sea. He described the figure as appearing to be in her thirties, with long, flowing hair and a look of deep sadness etched upon her face. Taniela and his fellow crew members believed the spirit to be that of one of the missing passengers, her soul forever bound to the vessel that had been her doom.

As the years passed and the MV Joyita continued to sail the waters of the Pacific, her haunted reputation only grew stronger. Tales of ghostly encounters and paranormal activity became an integral part of the vessel's lore, her story serving as a cautionary tale for those who would dare to venture into the unknown waters of the Pacific. The Joyita's chilling legacy would eventually come to an end in the 1960s, when the vessel was finally decommissioned and left to rot in a remote harbour, her once-proud form reduced to little more than a decaying relic of a bygone era.

The mystery of the MV Joyita and her vanishing ghost ship remains one of the most enduring enigmas in maritime history, a chilling reminder of the power and mystery of the sea. As we delve into the haunted histories and paranormal encounters that populate the pages of this book, we are reminded that there are forces at work in our world that defy explanation and that the ghosts of our past continue to cast their spectral shadows over the present.

The Young Teazer: The Fiery Spectre of Mahone Bay

As the sun sets over the calm waters of Mahone Bay, a fiery spectre is said to emerge from the depths, its ghostly form silhouetted against the darkening sky. For over a century, this eerie apparition has haunted the shores of Nova Scotia, casting its spectral shadow over the small coastal communities that dot the rugged landscape. Known as the Young Teazer, this doomed American privateer has become the stuff of local legend, its tragic explosion and subsequent ghostly sightings forever enshrined in the annals of maritime lore.

The story of the Young Teazer begins in the early 19th century, during the height of the War of 1812. Commissioned by the United States government to raid British shipping, the privateer set sail under the command of Captain William D. Dobson, a seasoned seafarer with a reputation for daring and cunning. Aboard the sleek and agile schooner, the crew of the Young

Teazer quickly made a name for themselves, their daring raids and audacious exploits striking fear into the hearts of British merchants and naval officers alike.

In June of 1813, the Young Teazer found herself pursued by a British squadron in the waters of Mahone Bay. Outnumbered and outgunned, Captain Dobson sought refuge in the bay's numerous coves and inlets, hoping to elude his pursuers and plot a daring escape. However, the British ships, led by the formidable HMS Hogue, were relentless in their pursuit, determined to bring the Young Teazer to heel and put an end to her reign of terror.

For several days, the two ships played a deadly game of cat and mouse amongst the fog-shrouded islands of Mahone Bay, the wily Captain Dobson using every trick in his arsenal to outwit and evade his adversaries. However, on June 27th, 1813, fate would deal the Young Teazer a cruel hand. Cornered by the HMS Hogue and her consorts, Captain Dobson found himself with little choice but to surrender or fight to the bitter end.

It was then that a terrible explosion tore through the night, the force of the blast lighting up the sky and shaking the very foundations of the earth. When the smoke cleared, all that remained of the Young Teazer were the scattered remnants of her once-proud form, her crew consigned to a watery grave in the cold, dark depths of Mahone Bay.

The exact cause of the explosion remains a matter of conjecture and debate. Some believe it to be the result of a desperate act of defiance by Captain Dobson, who chose to scuttle his ship rather than face capture and humiliation at the hands of the British. Others speculate that the blast was the result of a tragic accident, a stray spark igniting the vessel's powder magazine and sealing the fate of all aboard.

Regardless of the circumstances surrounding the Young Teazer's demise, her haunted legacy would live on in the form of a ghostly apparition said to rise from the waters of Mahone Bay on the anniversary of the tragic explosion. Known as the "Teazer Light," this eerie phenomenon has been reported by countless witnesses over the years, its fiery form drawing curious onlookers and paranormal enthusiasts from far and wide.

Many of those who have witnessed the Teazer Light describe it as an ethereal, flickering glow that seems to hover just above the surface of the water. Others claim to have seen the spectral form of a ship engulfed in flames, its ghostly crew standing at the rails, their tormented screams echoing across the bay. Some even assert that they have encountered the restless spirit of Captain Dobson himself, his ghostly figure wandering the shores of Mahone Bay in search of the crew he was unable to save from their terrible fate.

In the years since the tragic explosion, numerous theories have been put forward in an attempt to explain the mysterious Teazer Light. Some believe it to be the result of atmospheric phenomena or the reflection of distant lights on the water, while others contend that it is nothing more than the product of overactive imaginations and local folklore. However, for those who have witnessed the ghostly spectacle firsthand, there can be no doubt as to the supernatural origins of the eerie apparition.

Several accounts of close encounters with the Teazer Light have been documented over the years, their chilling details lending credence to the notion that the spirits of the Young Teazer and her crew continue to haunt the waters of Mahone Bay. One such story involves a local fisherman named Jonah McNeil, who claimed to have encountered the spectral ship while out on the water one fateful night in the early 1900s.

According to McNeil's account, he had been fishing alone in the bay when a sudden chill fell over the water, the temperature dropping precipitously as an eerie silence descended. It was then that he saw the Teazer Light, its ghostly glow casting an otherworldly pallor over the surrounding landscape. As the phantom ship approached, McNeil could make out the spectral figures of the crew, their faces etched with anguish and despair.

Unable to tear his eyes away from the horrifying spectacle, McNeil watched as the ghostly ship passed within mere feet of his tiny fishing boat, the air around him growing colder and colder as the apparition drew near. As the Teazer Light began to fade into the darkness, McNeil claims to have heard the haunting sound of a voice calling his name, the disembodied voice of Captain Dobson reaching out from beyond the grave.

Though McNeil's story is just one of many such tales that have been told over the years, it serves as a chilling reminder of the haunted legacy of the Young Teazer and her ill-fated crew. Despite the passage of time and the efforts of sceptics to dismiss the ghostly sightings as mere superstition, the Teazer Light continues to captivate the imagination and stir the hearts of those who live along the shores of Mahone Bay.

The tragic story of the Young Teazer and her fiery spectre has become an indelible part of the region's folklore and maritime history, a haunting reminder of the darker side of the sea and the restless spirits that are said to dwell within its depths.

The Eliza Battle: The Burning Ghost of the Tombigbee River

In the annals of haunted ships and maritime lore, few tales are as chilling and enduring as that of the Eliza Battle, a steamboat that once plied the waters of the Tombigbee River in the southern United States. Launched in 1852, the Eliza Battle was a state-of-the-art vessel for its time, boasting elegant accommodations and a reputation for safety and reliability. But in the years since her tragic demise, the Eliza Battle has become better known for her ghostly appearances on the very waters she once sailed, her spectral form eternally engulfed in flames.

To understand the haunting legacy of the Eliza Battle, we must first delve into the history of this remarkable vessel and the fateful events that led to her tragic end. Constructed in New Albany, Indiana, the Eliza Battle was a majestic side-wheel steamboat, measuring nearly 200 feet in length and capable of carrying up to 1,200 bales of cotton. For several years, the steamboat operated successfully along the Tombigbee River, transporting passengers and cargo between the bustling port cities of Mobile, Alabama, and Columbus, Mississippi.

The ill-fated journey that would forever seal the Eliza Battle's fate as a haunted vessel began on the evening of February 28, 1858, as the steamboat set off from Columbus with a full complement of passengers and crew. The ship was laden with cotton bales, a valuable cargo that would ultimately prove to be its undoing. As the Eliza Battle made its way down the Tombigbee River, the weather took a sudden and unexpected turn for the worse, with freezing temperatures and a fierce windstorm battering the vessel throughout the night.

It was in the midst of this violent tempest that disaster struck, as a fire broke out among the cotton bales on the steamboat's main deck. The flames spread quickly, fueled by the high winds and the highly flammable nature of the cargo. Despite the best efforts of the passengers and crew to extinguish the blaze, it soon became apparent that the Eliza Battle was doomed.

As the flames continued to consume the vessel, the passengers and crew were forced to abandon ship, leaping into the frigid waters of the Tombigbee River in a desperate bid for survival.

Tragically, many of those who managed to escape the inferno would succumb to hypothermia, their frozen bodies later discovered by search and rescue teams along the banks of the river. In total, more than 30 lives were lost in the disaster, making it one of the deadliest steamboat accidents in the history of the Tombigbee River.

In the years that followed the tragic demise of the Eliza Battle, rumours began to circulate of a ghostly steamboat seen aflame on the waters of the Tombigbee River, its spectral form appearing on cold and stormy nights reminiscent of the fateful evening in 1858. Witnesses claimed to have seen the burning ghost ship from the shore, its fiery image casting an eerie glow on the river's surface. Others spoke of encounters with the apparition while out on the water, their boats inexplicably drawn towards the phantom vessel as if caught in its ghostly wake.

Over time, the legend of the Eliza Battle and her haunting presence on the Tombigbee River has become an enduring part of local folklore, a chilling reminder of the steamboat's tragic history and the lives lost in the catastrophe. Numerous eyewitness accounts of the burning ghost ship have been documented, their chilling details painting a vivid picture of a vessel forever trapped in its final moments, its spectral crew and passengers eternally reliving the horror of that fateful night.

One such account comes from a fisherman named Silas Fletcher, who claimed to have witnessed the ghostly apparition of the Eliza Battle while out on the Tombigbee River one stormy night in the early 20th century. According to Fletcher, he had been struggling to navigate his small boat through the choppy waters when he suddenly noticed an eerie glow in the distance. As he drew closer, he could see the outline of a steamboat engulfed in flames, the vessel appearing to be in the throes of a desperate battle against the raging fire. Fletcher later recounted that he could hear the faint cries of passengers and crew emanating from the ghostly vessel, their voices carried on the wind like a haunting echo of the past.

Another harrowing encounter with the Eliza Battle comes from a group of riverboat workers in the 1930s, who claimed to have come face to face with the burning ghost ship during a particularly harsh winter. As they laboured to free their vessel from the ice that had trapped it on the Tombigbee River, the men suddenly found themselves enveloped in an eerie fog that seemed to materialise out of nowhere. It was within this shroud of mist that the phantom steamboat appeared, its fiery image casting an otherworldly light on the surrounding darkness. The terrified workers could do little but watch in awe as the Eliza Battle drifted past them, her spectral form eventually fading into the fog like a wisp of smoke.

In more recent years, sightings of the Eliza Battle have continued to be reported along the Tombigbee River, with witnesses describing the ghostly vessel as a terrifying yet mesmerising sight. Some have even claimed to see shadowy figures standing on the burning steamboat's deck, their spectral forms seemingly oblivious to the inferno that rages around them.

While sceptics may dismiss these accounts as mere folklore or the products of overactive imaginations, those who have experienced the haunting presence of the Eliza Battle firsthand remain convinced of the supernatural nature of the phenomenon. Some have even gone so far as to suggest that the ghostly steamboat serves as a spectral warning to those who dare to navigate the treacherous waters of the Tombigbee River, a chilling reminder of the perils that await those who underestimate the power of nature.

The Zebu: The Cursed Brigantine of the Mersey

For centuries, the Mersey River has been a bustling artery of maritime activity, its waters bearing witness to countless ships that have sailed along its winding course. Yet amidst the myriad vessels that have graced the Mersey, there is one ship whose haunted history and chilling paranormal encounters have earned it a place in the annals of nautical nightmares: the Zebu, a historic tall ship whose dark past and cursed reputation continue to shroud it in mystery.

Built in Sweden in 1938, the Zebu began its life as a humble cargo vessel, transporting goods and supplies throughout the Baltic Sea. However, it was not until the ship was purchased by a British merchant in the 1970s that its true destiny would be revealed. The new owner, captivated by the elegance and majesty of 19th-century sailing ships, decided to transform the Zebu into a traditional brigantine, complete with towering masts and billowing sails. Over the course of several years, the ship underwent an extensive restoration process, ultimately emerging as a stunning replica of a bygone era in maritime history.

Upon its completion, the Zebu quickly gained a reputation as one of the most striking tall ships on the Mersey, attracting visitors from far and wide who were eager to witness the vessel's beauty and grace. But as the ship's fame grew, so too did whispers of a darker side to the Zebu's story - a series of unsettling occurrences and inexplicable phenomena that seemed to suggest the presence of a malevolent force aboard the vessel.

The first inkling of the Zebu's haunted history came in the form of a tragic accident that occurred during the ship's restoration. According to eyewitness accounts, a young shipwright working on the vessel's rigging suddenly lost his footing and plummeted to his death, his body landing on the deck with a sickening thud. While such accidents were not entirely unheard of in the world of shipbuilding, the shipwright's demise was marred by an eerie coincidence: the man had reportedly been working on the very spot where a sailor had died in a similar accident over a century earlier.

As word of the shipwright's death spread, stories of other unsettling incidents aboard the Zebu began to surface. Crew members and visitors alike reported hearing strange sounds echoing throughout the ship - footsteps on the wooden deck when no one was near, whispered voices emanating from empty cabins, and the distant clang of chains as if an invisible crew were going about their duties.

Perhaps the most chilling of these accounts came from a night watchman who, while making his rounds on the Zebu, encountered a shadowy figure standing at the helm of the ship. As the watchman approached, the apparition turned to face him, revealing the spectral visage of a long-dead sailor before vanishing into thin air.

Intrigued by these tales of the supernatural, paranormal investigators began to delve into the Zebu's history, searching for clues that might explain the ghostly occurrences aboard the ship. What they uncovered was a series of tragic events and untimely deaths that seemed to have left an indelible mark on the vessel, imbuing it with an air of darkness and despair.

One such event was the death of a young cabin boy named Samuel, who perished aboard the ship in the early 1900s after being struck by a falling spar. As the story goes, the ship's captain, believing Samuel's death to be a bad omen, ordered that the boy's body be thrown overboard and his name stricken from the ship's log. But rather than appeasing the spirits, this act of callous disregard seemed only to intensify the hauntings, as if Samuel's restless spirit were seeking justice for his cruel and untimely fate.

Another tragic tale associated with the Zebu concerns a young couple who, having fallen in love aboard the ship, made the fateful decision to marry on its deck. As legend has it, the bride-to-be, dressed in her wedding gown, was ascending the stairs to the ship's deck when a sudden gust of wind caught her veil, pulling her over the side and into the dark waters of the Mersey. Despite the desperate efforts of her would-be husband and the ship's crew, the bride's body was never recovered, and her spirit is said to still haunt the Zebu to this day, her mournful wails echoing through the night air as she searches in vain for her lost love.

As these stories and others like them began to circulate, the Zebu's reputation as a cursed ship grew, drawing the attention of thrill-seekers and paranormal enthusiasts who flocked to the vessel in the hopes of catching a glimpse of its spectral inhabitants. While some of these visitors left disappointed, others found themselves confronted with spine-chilling encounters that seemed to defy explanation.

In one such incident, a group of tourists exploring the ship's lower decks claimed to have been chased by an unseen entity that rattled chains and pounded on the walls in a terrifying display of supernatural fury. In another, a woman who had strayed from her tour group found herself locked in a pitch-black cabin, her frantic cries for help drowned out by the eerie sounds of a ghostly crew going about their duties.

But of all the paranormal encounters reported aboard the Zebu, perhaps none is more famous than the legend of the ship's enigmatic captain, known simply as "Old Jack." Described as a grizzled, weather-beaten figure with piercing eyes and a mane of wild, unkempt hair, Old Jack is said to have been the captain of the original brigantine upon which the Zebu was modelled. According to legend, Old Jack's ship met a tragic end when it was caught in a fierce storm and dashed against the rocks, sending the vessel and its crew to a watery grave.

Yet rather than finding eternal rest in the depths of the ocean, Old Jack's spirit is said to have taken up residence aboard the

Zebu, watching over the ship with a stern and watchful eye. Some visitors to the Zebu have reported encountering Old Jack himself, who appears suddenly and without warning before vanishing just as quickly into the shadows.

The haunted history of the Zebu and the eerie encounters experienced by those who have ventured aboard the ship offer a chilling glimpse into the world of the supernatural, demonstrating the powerful hold that ghostly legends and tales of the paranormal can have on the human imagination. As the Zebu continues to sail the waters of the Mersey, its cursed reputation and ghostly inhabitants serve as a reminder of the darker side of maritime history - a world of tragedy, mystery, and restless spirits that linger long after the final voyage has come to an end.

The USS Constellation: The Haunted Heritage of Baltimore's Harbor

The majestic USS Constellation, anchored proudly in Baltimore's historic Inner Harbor, is a sight to behold. Launched in 1854, this impressive vessel stands as a testament to the United States Navy's rich maritime history. Today, the ship serves as a museum, allowing visitors to step back in time and experience life on a 19th-century warship. But as they explore its weathered decks and dimly lit passageways, some visitors have reported encountering more than just the echoes of the past. Whispered among the crew and patrons alike, the USS Constellation is said to harbour a host of ghostly spirits, forever bound to the ship they once served.

Among the numerous apparitions that have been sighted aboard the USS Constellation, one figure stands out in particular. The ghost of a former ship's captain, known only as Captain Thomas, is often seen roaming the decks and berthing compartments, keeping a watchful eye on his vessel from beyond the grave. Visitors have reported witnessing the captain's translucent figure, clad in a 19th-century naval uniform, silently observing the ship's activities. Some have even claimed to hear the faint sound of his boots on the wooden deck, echoing through the ship's darkened hallways.

Another spirit that is said to haunt the USS Constellation is that of a young sailor named Neil. Neil's tragic story begins when he fell ill during his time aboard the ship. As his health rapidly deteriorated, he was confined to the ship's sickbay, where he eventually succumbed to his illness. Since his untimely death, numerous visitors have reported encountering Neil's ghost, often appearing as a pale, gaunt figure with sunken eyes. Neil's spirit is said to be most active in the area where the sickbay was once located, and some have even claimed to hear the soft whispers of his voice, calling out to them from the shadows.

The ship's infirmary is also believed to be haunted by the spirit of a surgeon who once served aboard the Constellation. Known for his dedication to his work, the surgeon's ghost is said to be a benevolent presence, occasionally appearing to visitors and offering them a reassuring smile before vanishing into thin air. Some have even reported feeling a comforting touch on their shoulder or a gentle breeze, as if the surgeon's spirit is still tending to the well-being of those who venture into his domain.

One of the most chilling paranormal encounters reported aboard the USS Constellation took place in the ship's brig. A visitor, exploring the vessel on a guided tour, was shocked to discover a ghostly prisoner shackled to the wall of the small, dimly lit cell. The apparition appeared to be in great distress, moaning in agony and reaching out for help with his manacled hands. As the visitor backed away in terror, the tormented figure faded away, leaving behind only the chilling memory of the encounter.

As the sun sets and the shadows lengthen across Baltimore's harbour, the USS Constellation takes on an eerie atmosphere. The spirits that are said to inhabit the ship seem to become more active, as if drawn to the veil of darkness that envelops their timeless home. Visitors have reported the sensation of being watched, the sudden drop in temperature, and disembodied voices whispering in the wind as they navigate the ship's haunted decks.

The ghostly tales and supernatural sightings aboard the USS Constellation provide a captivating glimpse into the vessel's storied past, as well as the enduring fascination with the paranormal that continues to capture our imaginations. As you walk the decks of this historic ship, perhaps you, too, will feel the chill of a ghostly presence or hear the whispers of long-lost souls, beckoning you to uncover the mysteries that lie within the timeworn hull of the USS Constellation.

The haunted heritage of Baltimore's harbour, encapsulated by the USS Constellation, serves as a powerful reminder of the countless lives that have been touched by the sea and the remarkable stories that remain forever etched in its history. While the legends and paranormal encounters described in this chapter may defy explanation, they also provide a unique lens through which we can explore the depths of human curiosity, fascination, and connection to the past.

As you leave the USS Constellation and return to the bustling streets of Baltimore, the ghostly figures that are said to haunt its decks will continue to linger in the shadows, forever entwined with the ship's storied history. Their spectral presence serves as a haunting reminder that, in the words of an old maritime proverb, "The sea, once it casts its spell, holds one in its net of wonder forever."

With the ghostly tales and supernatural sightings of the USS Constellation, we add yet another captivating entry to the annals of haunted ships and boats that have enthralled seafarers and landlubbers alike for centuries. The mysteries and legends of these vessels serve as both a testament to the enduring allure of the paranormal and a haunting reminder of the profound impact that the sea has had on the course of human history.

Afterword

As we disembark from this chilling voyage through "Haunted Ships & Boats: Nautical Nightmares and Paranormal Encounters at Sea," we hope that your journey has been filled with intrigue, mystery, and an insatiable curiosity for the unknown. The ghostly tales of these 21 vessels have opened our eyes to the supernatural secrets that lie beneath the waves and offered a unique glimpse into the eerie allure of the sea.

The stories recounted in this book have spanned centuries, crossed oceans, and delved into the darkest corners of maritime history. Along the way, we've explored the human fascination with the paranormal and how it has fueled our desire to uncover the truth behind these mysterious phenomena. From tragic shipwrecks to unexplained disappearances, these haunted vessels continue to captivate our imagination and challenge our understanding of the world around us.

Although we've now reached the end of our nautical adventure, the mysteries surrounding these haunted ships and boats remain, inviting further exploration and inquiry. As you move forward, perhaps you'll be inspired to delve deeper into the world of the paranormal, seeking out more ghostly tales and unexplained phenomena that defy conventional explanation. And who knows, maybe one day you'll even find yourself aboard one of these legendary vessels, witnessing firsthand the eerie occurrences that have haunted generations of seafarers.

In the end, the stories of these haunted ships and boats serve as a reminder of the inexplicable nature of the world we live in and the eternal allure of the unknown. The ocean, with its vastness and depths, will forever remain a source of wonder and fascination, providing an endless canvas for human imagination and storytelling. As you close this book and return to the shores of your own reality, we hope that the chilling tales of these ghostly vessels continue to haunt your dreams and spark your curiosity for the mysteries that lie beneath the surface.

Thank you for joining us on this thrilling voyage into the world of nautical nightmares and paranormal encounters. As you navigate the waters of life, may you always maintain an open mind and an adventurous spirit, ready to embrace the unknown and uncover the extraordinary secrets that surround us.

Fair winds and following seas, fellow adventurers. Until our paths cross again in the realm of the supernatural.

Thank you for buying this book!

For more books in this series, search "Lee Brickley" on Amazon.

Printed in Great Britain
by Amazon